The Dance Technique of Doris Humphrey
AND ITS CREATIVE POTENTIAL

The Dance Technique of Doris Humphrey

AND ITS CREATIVE POTENTIAL

ERNESTINE STODELLE

Line Drawings by Teri Loren

PRINCETON BOOK COMPANY, PUBLISHERS
Princeton, New Jersey   1978

The photographs on pages 23 and 265 are by Barbara Morgan. The photographs on pages 77 through 233, 251, and 253 are by James Meehan. The photographs on pages 239, 242, 243, 254, and 255 are by Susan Perry. The frontispiece photograph is by Soichi Sunami.

Copyright © 1978 by
Princeton Book Company, Publishers
All rights reserved
Library of Congress Catalog Card Number 78-5124
ISBN 0-916622-07-X
Printed in the United States of America

Design by Emily Harste
Typography by Backes Graphics

To my colleagues of The Little Group
—Eleanor King, Letitia Ide, and José
Limón—with whom I first explored the
rich creative potential of Doris
Humphrey's technique.

E.S.

PREFACE

At first glance, the dance technique of Doris Humphrey, as presented and analyzed in this book, may appear to be surprisingly simple. After all, its theories are based on experiences which we all have every day and hour of our lives. For a healthy person, what is so difficult about breathing? For an energetic person, what is so amazing about "changing weight" as one walks or runs? And to a dancer, what is "Falling and Recovering" all about? Everyone knows that gravity rules our universe, that nothing is accomplished without coordination of mind and body, that our most ordinary gestures have purpose, conscious or unconscious. These are obvious and inescapable verities. Even the functioning mechanisms of one's body are taken for granted—if one is not a dancer, or a poet, or a philosopher, or a scientist.

Because Doris Humphrey was not only a dancer, but also a poet, a philosopher, and a scientist in spirit, she felt compelled to examine the fundamental realities of existence and to utilize them as the basis for a system of training which would serve, in turn, to express another kind of reality: the visions of the creative imagination. Never cold and calculating, but always emotionally and intellectually stimulated by her observations and experiences, Doris Humphrey created a technique to serve her creative purposes. It was not, however, a hard-core technique, but an elastic one with inspirational resources open to those who practiced it. "I always thought students should learn principles of movement and be encouraged to expand or embroider on these in their own way."[1] This is precisely why the dance technique of Doris Humphrey cannot be divorced from its creative potential.

To use this book most effectively as a teacher or a student, keep in mind that each exercise or study incorporates principles of movement which form the basis of Doris Humphrey's theories. Eloquence in terms of interpretation will assuredly follow, once the body has been trained to express itself in the Humphrey style. In teaching or performing the assignments, observe how the body best functions in the action so that an awareness of line and form will develop from *within*, rather than relying on the mirror image for accuracy.

The material throughout this book, with the exception of the last three spatial sequences which are drawn directly from compositions of Doris Humphrey, is geared for beginner and intermediate levels of study. The presentation follows the order of my own use of Doris Humphrey's technique: Center Work for basic, full body warm-up; Floor Work for concentrated leg, back, and center body stretching and strengthening; Barre Work for specialized training, not only in extensions and "turn-out," but also in the more demanding successional motions involved in falls, turns, etc.; and Spatial Sequences for complex coordinations to be found in large-scale traveling motions. There is an abundance of material in each section, to be selected and combined according to the student's needs as the lessons progress. The ultimate aim of this book is to provide today's aspiring dancers with the resources of a technique which, of itself, constitutes an original and unique vocabulary of movement. The reward of learning this vocabulary will be to confirm through one's body, mind, and feelings the truth of the incontestable logic that lies at the heart of Doris Humphrey's radiantly lyrical technique.

ACKNOWLEDGMENTS

In spite of the fact that I have based my lifetime teaching on the theories of Doris Humphrey, the idea of formulating and analyzing her principles for dance students in general came to me only after I had reconstructed her *Air for the G String* and *Two Ecstatic Themes* for the José Limón Dance Company in 1975. In recon-

[1] Doris Humphrey, *The Art of Making Dances* (New York: Rinehart & Co., 1959) p. 19.

structing these works, which were simultaneously recorded in Labanotation, I became aware of the necessity of training future interpreters of Humphrey compositions in the style of the dances they would perform. But more than that, the response of the Limon dancers to a master class I gave them at the time made me realize that the broad scope of the Humphrey Technique could provide today's modern dancers with enlightening means of developing their physical resources to the fullest, and, at the same time, release their creativity in ways that are unique. I am therefore indebted, first of all, to Ruth Currier, former Artistic Director of the José Limón Dance Company, for her desire to include two of Doris Humphrey's early works in the company's repertoire.

The dedicated participation of present members of my dance company—Gail Corbin, Estelle Gibbons, Penelope Hill, Margo Knis, Elizabeth Nimrod, Mira Pospisil—in the "expansion" of Doris Humphrey's inspiring ideas has made it possible for me to build the many studies and variations which serve as examples of the creative potential of the technique. Their whole-hearted allegiance, as well as that of former company members Carlotta Crissey, Rochelle Davis, Michelle Henthorn, Laura Wilson, and of my friend Eleanor Powers, has been, and still is, greatly prized.

A succinct reminder from Eleanor King, a charter member of the Doris Humphrey Concert Group, of the basic preparation for front falls was gratefully received just before I turned in the manuscript; Eleanor's total recall also made possible a reconstruction of the original *Water Study,* which I was able to present with the students of my 1976 Humphrey Technique Workshop at New York University.

In the writing of this book I have had valuable assistance from Edith White, whose sharp literary criticism struck time and again at vague and possibly confusing descriptions of movements analyzed in Part Two, *The Technique as Practice.* To my eldest daughter, Tanya K. Metaksa, and to my eldest sons, Christopher Komisarjevsky and Benedict Komisarjevsky, I am grateful for insights regarding the Prologue and the exposition of Doris Humphrey's philosophy and theories. And I want to thank Gloria and Marshall Litsky, who generously assumed responsibility for repeated typing and reproductions of the manuscript.

Although I did not have the privilege of dancing in Doris Humphrey's magnificent *Passacaglia,* it was a thrill to see some of the originally conceived movements performed by Anne Mac-

Naughton, who was in the premiere in 1938. Without her and Jennifer Muller's demonstrations, and without Lucy Venable's reminder of particulars in the execution, I could never have presumed to describe the two *Passacaglia* phrases which appear in the Spatial Sequences.

I am deeply indebted to Genevieve Oswald, Curator of the Dance Collection of the New York Public Library, and to her staff for the invaluable opportunity to study Doris Humphrey's copious notes and letters in quietude and at length. My special thanks goes to Andrew T. Wentink, whose splendid compilation and documentation of the Doris Humphrey Collection serves to provide others, like myself, with the means of penetrating retrospectively the mind and spirit of the great dancer-choreographer-theorist.

It is very unlikely that the shaping of the material of this book would have emerged in the form it has without the collaboration of Charles H. Woodford, Doris Humphrey's son. Charles's vision expanded my own by encouraging me to write detailed instructional descriptions of movements which were so ingrained in me as to be almost unconsciously experienced. To him I owe the effort of consciously trying to define them through the written word.

And lastly, without the steady encouragement of my husband, John Chamberlain, I doubt very much if this book would ever have materialized. His unwavering faith in my ability to write about the subject of my life's endeavors was always at hand to sustain me.

Ernestine Stodelle

Cheshire, Conn.
December, 1977

CONTENTS

Introduction, 39. SUCCESSIONS *1*. Successional Movement: Vertical, 39; *2*. Successional Movement: Sideways, 41; *3*. Sideways Succession with Drop and Gravitational Pull, 44. CHANGES OF WEIGHT *4*. Change of Weight with Falling Motion: Walking Version, 46; *5*. Change of Weight with Falling Motion: Single Step, 48. ISOLATIONS *6*. Shoulder Roll, 49; *7*. Head Roll,

Chapter 4   Floor Work   103

Chapter 5   Barre Work   169

Now is the time for me to tell of the nobility
that the human spirit is capable of, stress the
grace that is in us, give the young dancers a
chance to move harmoniously with each other . . . .
    Doris Humphrey, *1943*

Prologue
A PERSONAL REMINISCENCE

The atmosphere at 9 East 59th Street was dramatically simple. A very small, rather dark area like a vestibule greeted the newcomer to the fifth floor studio of Doris Humphrey and Charles Weidman; but almost immediately one came into a large, empty rectangular room with light streaming in from tall windows facing south on 59th Street. The grandeur of that starkly bare space was impressive.

Perhaps the studio was not as large as I now visualize it; perhaps the entrance room leading to it was not as small or as dark as my memory pictures it. Feelings have a way of expanding or contracting reality to measure up (or down) to the spirit's needs. All I know now—with certainty—is that I, a girl just turned seventeen and having been given eighteen dollars as a high school graduation present, was obeying the strongest impulse of my young life: to study with, and identify with, two of America's greatest artists, Doris Humphrey and Charles Weidman.

Eighteen dollars would pay for nine lessons during that June of 1929, nine marvelous lessons to steep myself in before leaving to spend the summer at a camp, where I had been engaged to teach dancing. My previous study of classical ballet and my more recent experience in Denishawn technique for one year with Denishawn graduate Ruth Jentzer in Brooklyn had fitted me, in the eyes of the camp director, for the job. But I was looking far beyond the summer. I had seen Doris Humphrey and Charles

1

Weidman and their Concert Group perform the preceding October at the Civic Repertory Theatre on West 14th Street. Since that moment I knew without a doubt where I must go and what I must do to prepare myself for the supreme task of trying to dance as they did.

The high ceilings, the pearl-grey studio walls—free of mirrors or pictures—and the glistening parquet floor gave the room I entered a quiet elegance. Grey, too, was the color of Doris Humphrey's teaching costume: a crepe-textured short-sleeved dress that fit snugly over the torso with a folded, center-split skirt that hung straight from her narrow hips. It was a costume made to reveal the body, free the arms, and disclose the constantly varied motions of the legs. With her voluminous light auburn hair caught back loosely with a coronet-like ribbon, her aristocratic, chiseled features, Doris stood before me, a vision of everything a dancer should be: perfectly proportioned, slender, romantically beautiful. Then this vision began to speak.

In the recesses of my consciousness I still hear that eloquent voice with its warm, rich tones and the clearly enunciated words that conjured up a whole universe of ideas which my mind leapt at eagerly. Ethereal as she might seem to be, this young woman of thirty-three was solidly aware of reality as concrete experience upon which she hoped to build whole theories of movement. Not for her the self-indulgence of emotional outbursts; not for her the purely impulsive gesture. The why and the how of human action[1], of man's relation to his environment (in those years, to his natural environment, not to his social condition), these were the vital subjects of her concern. How well I remember feeling that sudden recognition of elementary truth when Doris spoke of balance in terms of "oppositional" movement, of rhythm as grouped pulsations in time, of space as containing three spheres of motion—air, water, earth—and six basic directions—forward, back, sideways, up, down, and around.

Something in me began to rise and assert itself in response to these clear-cut statements. Since childhood my love of poetry and fairy tales had been offset by a deep curiosity about factual experience. I filled notebooks with questions whose answers I daringly conjectured. At the age of fourteen, Einstein's Theory of

---

[1] "A movement without a motivation is unthinkable." Doris Humphrey, *The Art of Making Dances* (New York: Rinehart, 1959), p. 110.

Relativity fascinated me. Not that I understood everything I read, but such books, along with records of symphonic music which I found in abundance in a superbly stocked library of an uncle of mine, provided an escape into a world where imagination and "scientific" conclusions moved in tandem. When Doris Humphrey stood before me and analyzed human movement, beauty and logic coalesced. No longer separate, warring truths, they became one living entity, nourishing each other like the heart and the head.

Nine lessons did not, of course, provide me with the basic secrets of how to dance like the members of the Concert Group. But those nine lessons, several of which were taught by Charles Weidman, whose personality and talent captivated all of us, strengthened my resolve to make dancing in the Humphrey style the goal of my life. Come late September, I would be back at 9 East 59th Street, ready to devote myself to these ideals without cease. I was already painfully aware of the faults which my teachers had pointed out. Doris immediately spotted rhythmic inaccuracies in my rough attempts to follow instructions; and Charles's repeated reprimands of "Too much, too much, Ernestine!" forced me to hold back some of the energy that seemed to possess me as soon as I started to dance. Lest I be discouraged, that compassionate man would add, "Well, too much is better than not enough."

Three months later, with even greater enthusiasm, I returned. My friend, Sylvia Manning (one of the leading members of the Group with whom I had had the good fortune to become acquainted at Ruth Jentzer's studio[1]) was deep in rehearsals, which took place in the evenings, but I saw her frequently when I came to class. Another girl about my own age started lessons that fall as well. Her name was Letitia Ide.

At the beginning of November, Letitia and I each received from Doris a lengthy hand-written "letter to a prospective member of the Group." With scrupulous zeal I copied my letter into my notebook. Each word seemed weighed for clarity, so as not to misrepresent facts or give the reader false impressions. At the same time, the text frankly acquainted the recipient with the aspirations of the author:

. . . so my aims may be summed up like this—I am first a crea-

---

[1] Sylvia Manning danced the central role in the premiere and subsequent performances of *Air for the G String*. Doris Humphrey performed that role for the first and last time in the 1934 film of the work.

tive artist, thirsting to see my conceptions made visible. After that I am also interested in developing individual talent in others, educating audiences, performing for audiences, promoting the cause of the Dance, making money and establishing a Dance Theatre in America . . . . There is much more, but I think the most important aspects are covered here. I hope you will understand from this brief explanation what my ideas are and my ambition for the group, and will consider seriously and long whether you would like to cast your lot with us.

Though I did not consider it unusual at the time that Doris should write to us rather than speak to us personally, I realized later how true to form she had acted. There had been disappointments regarding one or two members of the company, and Doris, being a realist, was not willing to subject herself to further misunderstandings. Her letter strove to make us comprehend the full responsibility of our actions should we decide to join these two dedicated artists in their quest for a dance of their own devising.

It soon became apparent to those of us who came regularly to the 59th-Street studio in the fall of 1929 that there was a third person who was equally dedicated to the ideals described in Doris's communiqué. From her place at the small lamp-lighted table in the vestibule where she spoke to prospective students and took tuition fees, or from behind the keyboard of the grand piano as she played for classes, Pauline Lawrence exerted undeniable influence on everything that was going on. A plump, dark-haired, observant woman, she had a sharp eye for detecting talent.[1]

Musician (singer, pianist, accordionist), costume and lighting designer, first-rate seamstress, and business manager par excellence, Pauline possessed yet another gift: an astonishing ability to estimate a given situation accurately, whether it involved an esthetic or practical problem. In her realistic motherly way, she guided the careers of Doris Humphrey and Charles Weidman through one of

---

[1] No doubt it was Pauline who first took the measure of the tall, big-boned Mexican youth who came into class. His name was José Limón. With his heart-warming smile and bullish enthusiasm, he was far too animated, far too awkward for the comfort of those who might be dancing next to him. If you let on that he pulled you too violently, José would be overcome with remorse, and all his Spanish-bred chivalry would rise to make amends.

the most precarious periods of their joint professional lives. We all sensed Pauline's captainship and respected her profoundly.

At that time, even after we had moved from 59th Street to the third-story loft at 151 West 18th Street in late 1930, Doris's major concern was her ensemble choreography, not the creation of a basic technique. Of course, theories for such a technique were constantly simmering in her mind; but the truth was that she had not yet formulated any satisfactory answers to her own investigations. Very shortly, however, circumstances obliged her to come to grips with the problem. In January, 1931, a series of lecture-demonstrations was to be inaugurated for the purpose of acquainting the general public with the philosophies and achievements of the leading figures in the burgeoning art of modern dance. John Martin, dance critic of the *New York Times,* was to chair the events, which were to be shared by Doris Humphrey and Martha Graham. (In subsequent years, the series was expanded to include other outstanding modern dance exponents.) The locale for the presentations was the Lecture Room of the New School for Social Research, which had just opened its doors on West 12th Street.

The format of the lecture-demonstration challenged Doris to evaluate more critically her previous investigations and, just as important, to put her conclusions to work as demonstrable action. She took up the challenge with characteristic daring, but, with characteristic honesty, she admitted (in a letter to her parents postmarked January 17, 1931,[1] the week of her first lecture) some unsettling doubts:

> After some twenty years of working and thinking I'm still not sure of much of anything . . . You know, I have completely reconstructed my ideas of the dance in the years [since] I left Denishawn . . . I'm groping for a new approach . . . I teach only one class this year—and even that is irksome mostly because I have never made up my mind how to do it. Isn't that silly? I've decided that I really have no particular talent for analysis—or it wouldn't come so hard [!]. Anyway, I'm straining my wits to try to present my work not only logically but attractively . . . .

The deadline worked its magic. Our classroom material, based

---

[1] Humphrey, Doris. Doris Humphrey Collection. 1811-1958. Folder C-283. (New York Public Library. Research Library of the Performing Arts. The Dance Collection.) Hereafter referred to as the Doris Humphrey Collection.

on our director's early explorations of natural movement as a viable basis of a theory, was stripped of extraneous experimentation, redefined, and refocused to prove elementary points concerning balance, momentum, direction, and so on. Then a subtle transformation took place. A dance form only hinted at in the classroom emerged: the Study. With seemingly unlimited choreographic inventiveness, Doris created studies in rhythm, in oppositional and successional movement, studies in the varying dynamics of falling, studies in walking, running, and leaping. All of them were pure movement compositions, superbly crafted examples of her double gift of analysis and creativity.

Years later, when describing her approach to natural movement as a basis for technique, Doris wrote revealingly about her use of the Study: "Because they [natural movements] sprang so truly and psychologically from physical life, they were emotionally stirring even without a program. This characteristic led me to compose a number of dance studies and even dance compositions entirely without a dramatic idea."[1] The New School for Social Research series not only provided an incentive but also a suitable setting for the trial-and-error exposure of such explorations and discoveries.

The room in which the lecture-demonstrations took place was downstairs, beneath the school's street-level auditorium. The performing area was circular and sunk into the center of the room. As the audience was seated in a broad semi-circle facing and flanking us, our presentation was practically "in the round." After John Martin's introduction, Doris would describe her philosophy and its theories while we sat informally in practice clothes on the curved steps behind her. At the conclusion of our demonstrations, Martin would offer the public a question-and-answer period. When this took place, we would resume our positions on the steps and would listen with great interest while Doris, still standing, "defended" her philosophy. Actually, I relished those final moments of discussion. Having started teaching on my own, I was likewise imbued with the evangelistic spirit of educating audiences to the esthetic of the new dance.

One or two other girls in the company were also obliged to teach as a means of earning a living. Performances were very infre-

[1]Humphrey, "My Approach to the Modern Dance" (IN: Frederick Rand Rogers ed., *Dance: A Basic Educational Technique.* New York: Macmillan, 1941), p. 190.

quent, and they paid a mere ten dollars apiece. But in those Depression times even a teaching job was hard to come by, unless one opened a studio of one's own, as I did in New Haven, Connecticut. Some of the Group members existed by posing for artists and sculptors (at one dollar per hour), and a few were waitresses in small downtown restaurants. We had to settle for part-time work; rehearsals were in the evenings, and, occasionally, costume fittings or special assignments occurred during the day. And there were other, more subtle responsibilities, voluntarily assumed: reading books of philosophy and poetry; being conversant with contemporary literature; going to music concerts and art museums. Self-cultivation was part of the process of growing into a truly distinctive modern dancer; that was understood from the beginning.

But whatever the daily tasks, when seven o'clock came on rehearsal night, we would effortlessly climb the two long flights of wooden steps leading to the whitewashed brick loft in happy anticipation of the coming three-hour rehearsal. The studio was surprisingly quiet now that the shoe-and machine-shop factories on the lower floors were closed for the night. With darkness behind them, the four big skylights over the room's central area seemed to contain mysterious flickerings of light as we danced beneath them. The rehearsal space itself was square, but near the entrance, a catty-cornered platform held chairs for visitors.[1] In the other corner stood the grand piano, the only reminder of the 59th Street studio. There were no barres in the loft, walls served for support when ballet exercises were performed.[2] Doris directed from the front, springing up periodically from her place on a bench or chair between the entrance and dressing-room doors.

A single, narrow mirror hung behind the visitors' chairs. It was used very seldom, and then only to check out body designs. I remember José using it when he composed his *Danza*, a brilliant solo which was premiered in one of our "Little Group" performances. (The Little Group was originally planned for a six-member

---

[1] I remember Doris's husband "Leo" (whose name was Charles, but Doris distinguished him from her partner by this affectionate nickname) sitting in the visitors' "corner," watching us intently through many a long rehearsal.

[2] The only instances of doing ballet exercises which I recall were when we started rehearsing for *The School for Husbands*, a Theatre Guild production of Molière's saucy comedy. Doris and Charles were engaged to choreograph ballet interludes and to dance in a fantasy episode entitled, "The Dream of Sganarelle." It was in 1933, one year after we had been performing *Shakers* and *Water Study* with great success in the Broadway revue *Americana*.

company to operate independently within the context of the Humphrey-Weidman Company. It soon simmered down to four: Eleanor King, Letitia Ide, José Limón and myself. Doris and Charles encouraged us to perform our own works, and naturally offered criticism. Pauline often designed our costumes. With tentative hopes and shaky legs we would present our fledgling dances to our revered directors, whose opinions never failed to shake us up still further.)[1]

The big moments in the studio came when Doris would start a new work; the most memorable for me was when she told us her ideas for *Dionysiaques.* It was afternoon or early evening, and the light was especially kind to the plain, workaday atmosphere of the loft. Doris, wearing street clothes, had in her hands a large, flat book entitled *The Palace at Knossos.* It contained many remarkable photographs, some in color, of Crete's ancient civilization, the ruins of which were still preserved on the island.

Grouping ourselves around her in the visitors' corner, we studied the book while Doris slowly turned the pages. Then she began to describe the dance she had in mind. Its theme would be a reenactment of an ancient Cretan rite: the yearly propitiation of the Bull God by sacrificing the most important personage in the community, the High Priestess. The sacrifice, to be depicted on-stage, would take the form of a fall from a great height into, presumably, a deep lake. The ballet would be cast for all the women in the Group plus two men, José Limón and Gene Martel; Doris herself would dance the leading role.

Whenever Doris described her ideas they were vividly clear, for she had thought them through over a long period and could conjure up a scene with the most telling words. Even the choreography could be visualized to some degree. As she played the music she had selected, Florent Schmitt's composition for band, *Dionysiaques,* the dance she had pictured seemed to unfold. It was rhythmically exciting music, martial at moments, thin and wailing at others, and then, just before the end, wildly dissonant.

Performing *Dionysiaques* proved to be a thrilling experience; but I don't think that any of us realized at the time the enormous

[1]Charles's verdict of Eleanor's highly original idea for three dances from Peter Warlock's adaptation of the sixteenth century *Capriol Suite* was disturbingly frank. He called our light-touch comedy in *Dances for Saturday, Sunday and Monday* "raw meat," a criticism that did not hinder us from performing the trio extensively. Doris was more encouraging, though somewhat noncommittal after watching José's and my duet, *Tango,* which had a percussion accompaniment. "Well, all I can say is," she remarked with a wan smile, "it's a primitive sex dance."

importance of the ballet as a stimulant to Doris's creative powers. Philosophically, *Dionysiaques* expressed the eternal conflict and resolution of the Apollonian-Dionysian elements in man, a psychological counterpoint described by Friedrich Nietzsche in his *Birth of Tragedy*. Technically, *Dionysiaques* used balance and imbalance, the elements of Doris's principles of Fall and Recovery, as later formulated in "The Arc Between Two Deaths."[1] Prophetically, *Dionysiaques* served as the groundwork for the "new approach" that Doris was groping for: one that would satisfy her both as philosophy and technique. That she was already aware of her commitment to the Apollonian-Dionysian concept of movement-incentive is evident in a letter she wrote to her parents shortly after the premiere of the ballet in April, 1932:

> The *Dionysiaques,* you might like to know, was inspired by a reading of Nietzsche's *Birth of Tragedy* last summer . . . and in fact [it] has greatly influenced my whole approach to dancing.[2]

Later statements, experiments, and examples—theatrical as well as theoretical—bear testimony to Doris's creative use of the Nietzschean philosophy as confirmation of her own probings into the characteristics of natural movement. While the themes of future dances[3] were concerned with a variety of subjects, the rhythmic and dynamic aspects of the movement configurations in all of Doris's compositions prove to be evolutionary products of the Fall and Recovery principles explored in 1931-1932.

It was my good fortune to have been a member of the Doris Humphrey and Charles Weidman Concert Group, which later became the Humphrey-Weidman Company, during those formulative years. When I left in May, 1935, a new choreographic era was about to begin. But already the main investigatory work had been launched and the Humphrey Technique had evolved into the style of movement for which it is now renowned.

This book attempts to offer a comprehensive study of Doris Humphrey's use of Nietzsche's Apollonian-Dionysian concept in relation to the principles underlying her technique. These principles will be analyzed and explored in exercises and studies that constitute a basic training in the Humphrey style; they will also

[1] Humphrey, *The Art of Making Dances,* p. 106.
[2] Doris Humphrey Collection. Folder C-300.
[3] Those composed for the Humphrey-Weidman Company, as well as those composed for the José Limón Dance Company and the Juilliard Dance Theatre until her death in 1958.

serve as inspirational points of departure for suggested creative use of an approach to dance, which has universal implications.

A description in the Epilogue of those early works which are, to my mind, most vividly expressive of my former director's theories will, I trust, shed further light on the creative discoveries of a great artist, whose choreographic and educational contributions to American dance are of inestimable historical and practical value.

PART ONE

THE BACKGROUND OF THE TECHNIQUE

"To view science through the optics of the artist,
and art . . . through the optics of life."
Friedrich Nietzsche, *The Birth of Tragedy*

Chapter 1
THE TECHNIQUE AS PHILOSOPHY

Nietzsche was the catalyst, providing Doris Humphrey with the broad-schemed philosophy that justified and clarified all her preliminary probings into natural movement as a basis for dance technique. Nietzsche was the creative stimulant for ideas not yet formulated but already imbedded in a personality given to studious speculation. For Doris Humphrey, like the great nineteenth-century German philosopher, was a philologist, a scholar. She loved learning not only for its own sake, but also for the illuminations it shed on mankind in general.

A purely personal approach to movement would never have satisfied this extraordinary woman with the enquiring mind. One has only to study the copious notes she wrote in preparation for lectures, classes, interviews, and extended writing to realize how her search into the motivations and behavior of human action went far beyond personal experience. Philosophic in her powers of deduction, scientific in her powers of analysis, and poetic in her powers of expression, Doris Humphrey examined and reexamined the process of life in nature and man:

> If we understand in our bodies the various ways that force moves and the various sequences that it moves in we know something about ourselves because we all as an organism follow the same laws.[1]

[1] Doris Humphrey Collection. Folder M-66.

Force (energy) is investigated as a creative element in itself:

The desire to move stimulates organic matter to reach out from its center of equilibrium. But the desire to maintain life stimulates a return to equilibrium or another reaching out of matter sufficient to balance the first, and so save the organism from destruction.[1]

Equilibrium/destruction. Polar states, which, as Doris Humphrey investigates further, are sustained through the pulsating properties of rhythm:

Hence, rhythm results from the oscillation of organic matter moving away from and back to its point of equilibrium. . .[2]

Working logically from the same scientific base, she perceives the ultimate effect:

At either end of the movement there is death—the static death or constant equilibrium or the dynamic death in too extreme movement away from equilibrium.[3]

Static death/dynamic death. We have but to convert the phrase "organic matter" into its human equivalent—Man—to anticipate the inevitable conclusion: Motion between these two "deaths" represents nothing more nor less than the struggle to survive.

Small wonder that Nietzsche's audacious attempt, in *The Birth of Tragedy,* "to view science through the optics of the artist, and art . . . through the optics of life"[4] struck Doris Humphrey so forcibly. She, too, was an observer of nature. She, too, peered at science though the lens of her sensibilities; she, too, produced art as a revelation of life. Small wonder that Nietzsche's analysis of pre-Christian Greek culture, as expressed in his Apollonian-Dionysian thesis of extremes, provided the clue for Doris Humphrey's philosophy of motion in her concept of "The Arc Between Two Deaths." The double image served her perfectly.

According to Nietzsche, the art-deities Apollo and Dionysus represented two conflicting, yet intertwining impulses in man: the first, to achieve perfection and stability; the second, to experience

[1] Doris Humphrey Collection. Folder M-65.
[2] Doris Humphrey Collection. Folder M-65.
[3] Doris Humphrey Collection. Folder M-65.
[4] Friedrich Nietzsche, *The Birth of Tragedy*, trans. Wm. A. Haussmann (New York: Macmillan, 1924), p. 4.

the ecstacy of abandon. Apollo, god of wisdom and light, "rules over the fair appearance of the inner world of fantasies" with "measured limitation . . . freedom from the wilder emotions . . . philosophical calmness . . . ."[1] Dionysus, god of wine, song, dance, and drama, releases man's instinct for adventure, for danger: "Under the influence of the narcotic draught . . . Dionysian emotions awake . . . [and] the subjective vanishes to complete self-forgetfulness."[2] No longer plagued by his moral conscience, man "is on the point of taking a dancing flight into the air . . . he feels himself a god . . . ."[3]

Translate Dionysian licentiousness to the precarious state of off-balance motion, and you will encounter the imminent danger of "dynamic death." Translate Apollonian serenity into the security of symmetrical balance, and you will have the locked-in perfection of "static death." Translate the rhythmic "oscillation of organic matter" into the living arc between these two deaths, and you have the Humphrey principle of "Falling and Recovering."

"Dionysian and Apollonian . . . are different names for the will to grow and the will to balance,"[4] wrote Doris Humphrey. The psychological counterpoint emerges. Growth is an outward reaching, a tempting of fate, a daring act of exploration leading to self-knowledge or disaster. Balance implies rational behavior, clear judgment, but is in danger of stultification. The psyche vacillates, lured irresistibly in opposite directions.

Falling and recovering is the very stuff of movement, the constant flux which is going on in every living body, in all its tiniest parts, all the time. Nor is this all, for the process has a psychological meaning as well. I recognized these emotional overtones very early and instinctively responded very strongly to the exciting danger of the fall, and the repose and peace of recovery.[5]

Excitement/repose. Danger/peace. The dichotomy expands. Within the ninety-degree arc between the body upright in fixed equilibrium and the body lifelessly prone lies an infinity of action, emotional as well as physical. Just as there is delight in danger, there is terror in danger; just as there is peace in repose, there is

[1] Nietzsche, *The Birth of Tragedy*, pp. 23-24.
[2] Nietzsche, *The Birth of Tragedy*, p. 25.
[3] Nietzsche, *The Birth of Tragedy*, pp. 26-27.
[4] Doris Humphrey Collection. Folder M-65.
[5] Humphrey, "My Approach to the Modern Dance," p. 189.

deathly stillness for the spirit in repose. To fall is to yield; to recover is to reaffirm one's power over gravity and oneself.

. . . forever opposed and existing both in one man and in groups of men, the *Apollonian* and the *Dionysian* are the symbols of man's struggle for progress on the one hand, and his desire for stability on the other hand. These are not only the basis of Greek tragedy, as Nietzsche pointed out, but of all dramatic movement, particularly dance.[1]

To dream of perfection, and to court danger. Herein lies the dual nature of man, and the rich creative potential of the Humphrey Technique.

---

[1] Humphrey, "My Approach to the Modern Dance," p. 189.

Chapter 2
THE TECHNIQUE AS THEORY

Since my dance is concerned with immediate human values,
my basic technique lies in the natural movements of the human body.
  Doris Humphrey, *My Approach to the Modern Dance*

From such basic acts as breathing, standing, walking, running, leaping, rising, and falling came the inspiration for Doris Humphrey's theories of movement. Simple as these fundamental human motions appear to be, they contain the ever-present drama of man's struggle to gain mastery over himself and his physical environment.

When Doris Humphrey speaks of natural movement, she is referring to forces inherent in nature as well as in man. In her study of elemental motion, she recognized that action is followed by reaction, that force is counteracted by force. The "natural movements of the human body" are the visible evidence of man's ability to survive in a world dominated by gravity. At times his friend, at times his foe, gravitational force imposes itself upon every move he makes. "All life fluctuates between resistance to and yielding to gravity."[1]

In this sense, the Humphrey Technique is a continuous exploration of movement as physiological-psychological experience. Not only does the Humphrey approach to natural movement accept the dramatic reality of human coexistence with gravity, it builds its entire esthetic on elements of motion underlying that coexistence. These elements constitute the principles of movement

[1] Humphrey, *The Art of Making Dances*, p. 106.

17

on which the technique is based: Falling and Recovering, Successional Flow, Breath Rhythms, Oppositional Motion, and Change of Weight. Woven into these principles—and used consciously in the classroom as working ingredients of the technique— is the founder's comprehensive analysis of Rhythm, Dynamics (Quality of Motion), and Design. The style of dance that emerges is, in essence, lyrical. It expresses the innate power of the human spirit to triumph over adverse forces.

Whereas other established dance techniques train the body by means of a specific code of graduated exercises from the simple to the complex, the Humphrey Technique concentrates on the *movement experience* throughout the developmental procedure. "Since the dance is kinetic, not primarily literary, dramatic or musical . . . Training should aim first at feeling for movement in design, in rhythm, in quality."[1] For example, stretches, body bends, leg swings, thigh and foot exercises, jumps, leaps, falls, and so on, are rhythmically and dynamically phrased. In addition, there is emphasis on sensing the forms as a design that these motions create. A further distinction lies in the fact that these exercises are, in many instances, "choreographically" arranged. Instead of patterned positions repetitiously performed, whole sequences of movements are thematically developed, much in the manner of a dance composition. The kinetic impulse has been explored through a reshaping and timing of the natural rhythms and dynamics inherent in the movement idea. When performing these miniature "studies," the student gains insight into the *choreographic potential* of the Humphrey Technique, a stimulating experience for the initiate.

Thus it can be said that the Humphrey Technique, which comprises Doris Humphrey's philosophy of dance and its unique movement style, has two major aims: 1. to develop bodily strength, flexibility, control, and endurance—in short, the necessary skills for performing; and 2. to encourage the student toward creative use of the principles of movement through experiential understanding of their rhythmic, dynamic, and design potentials. A dual approach such as this steers the classroom experience directly onto the stage, the stage of the dancer's imagination, where dances are born. "By knowing which movements will be most stimulat-

---

[1] Doris Humphrey Collection. Folder M-37.

ing, the dance can arrive at the desired state, the feeling of drama in motion. . . ."[1]

What greater drama could there be than that of falling? Falling from the security of perfect balance, falling from grace, falling in love. In the fall from Apollonian symmetry, man experiences the intoxication of abandon; he probes the delights of the *danger zone,* where Dionysian ecstacy comes close to death. Intrinsically bound up with the body's relationship to universal laws of physics, Falling and Recovering permeates every action within the framework of the Humphrey Technique. It sets up a subtle interweaving of physical timing and psychological response; it establishes various degrees of intensity, which Doris Humphrey called "quality of movement." Dynamic motion, as represented by the body's constantly changing reactions to gravitational pull, reveals the behavior of the nervous system. "Movement is a neuro-musculo-skeletal event. The nervous system initiates movement and controls its patterning."[2]

Beginning with the all-inclusive Falling and Recovering theory, let us examine the movements upon which the principles of the Humphrey Technique are based. Breathing, Standing, Change of Weight, Walking, Running, and Leaping will each be analyzed in the context of its natural functions, and then in respect to its creative potential as dance experience.

From unpublished notes[3] we have Doris Humphrey's own analysis of this germinating principle:

FALLING AND RECOVERING AS FUNDAMENTAL EXPERIENCE

The story of my technique is very simple. I came back to the body and its proclivities for movements, and tried to divorce it from all sorts of emotional reactions—what will the body do by itself? What proclivities does it have for balance? What happens when it moves? How does it change to maintain balance? The very first thing I discovered was that the body's natural, instantaneous movement—its very first movement, is a falling movement. If you stand perfectly still and do not try to control the movement, you will find that you will begin to fall in

[1] Doris Humphrey Collection. Folder M-37.
[2] Lulu E. Sweigard, *Human Movement Potential* (New York: Dodd, Mead, 1975), p. 3.
[3] Collection of Charles H. Woodford.

one direction. You will fall forward or, probably backward, because you have less to hold you up. This seemed to be a very simple discovery, and yet a tremendously important one, if you're going to start a new technique based on body movement.

FALLING AND RECOVERING AS DANCE EXPERIENCE

A movement-phrase in three parts, the act of Falling and Recovering can be experienced "vertically" through the body in the sense that the dancer remains in one place and sinks to the floor, falling downward and recovering upward; or "radially" in the sense that as the dancer moves through space, the falling/recovering motif is the central ingredient of the action. In practicing the rhythmic timing of the falling/recovering movement, it is suggested that the dancer use the breath as described below.

Fall—Rebound—Suspension

Part 1: Fall. From the static point of poised equilibrium, the body begins to fall, slowly at first, and then with accelerating speed as it succumbs to gravitational pull. The direction may be forward, backward, spiral, or sideways. In the process of falling, the breath is gradually expelled.

Part 2: Rebound. When collapse is imminent, a self-protective mechanism goes into action (provided the fall is not intended to be completed or is accidental), and a counter movement takes place in which the body springs back as if with renewed life. This *rebound,* which is similar in motion to that of a ball bouncing upward or outward from a hard surface, is rapid at first, decelerating as it rises. At the moment of rebound, the breath is inhaled sharply; as the body begins to recover equilibrium, the breath fills the lungs.

Part 3: Suspension. At this point, the rebound has entered the state of suspension, which is the transitory stage of the body momentarily supporting itself off-balance before returning to equilibrium. In terms of physics, energy has reached "the point of zero" (because there is no oscillation); in terms of dance experience, the body is poised triumphantly midair having successfully recovered from the perils of falling.

BREATHING AS FUNDAMENTAL EXPERIENCE

With the intake of the breath, the entire body is nourished. "To breathe is life. Without breath we die. To breathe rhythmically is health."[1] Partly unconscious, the act of breathing has its own dynamic phrasing, which is related through diaphragmatic action to the organic and skeletal rhythms of the body.

BREATHING AS DANCE EXPERIENCE

If we analyze breathing in dance terms we can visualize the breath successively moving from the torso to the extremities. Inhalation is the initial force; the flow follows the pattern of radiating energy from the body's center, upward into the neck and head, downward into the legs, and outward into the arms and hands. With exhalation, the successional direction of breath flow (as dance) is reversed: the torso, releasing its energies, sinks downward and inward; the extended arms, which reached their full stretch through the successive manipulation of the elbows, wrists, hands, and fingers, now retract in the same order, but in the direction of the body.

Successional Flow, one of the principles of Doris Humphrey's theories of natural movement, may be cited to describe the imagined route of breath flow. The dancer, aware of the energizing power of the breath, may choose to utilize successional motion to convey an illusion of the act of inhalation and exhalation. It should be understood that when performing, the dancer does not consciously coordinate the breath with the movement, though such coordinations may be practiced in the classroom. Breath and movement are simultaneous, but not necessarily conjunctive dance actions.

By its very nature, breathing establishes a "phrase rhythm" which reshapes movement, endowing it with varying intensities and forms:

> In the dance, we can use the simple rise and fall of the breath in its original location in the chest, but this is by no means all. The idea of breath rhythm—the inhalation, suspension and ex-

---

[1] Mabel Elsworth Todd, *The Thinking Body* (Paul B. Hoeber, 1937. Reprint: Brooklyn, N.Y., Dance Horizons, 1972), p. 217.

halation—can be transferred to other parts of the body. One can "breathe" with the knees, or the arms, or the whole body . . . These breath rhythms are subject to the most infinite variety as to parts of the body, shorter or longer timing, and various uses of space . . . There is a whole world of movement implicit in just this part of rhythm.[1]

A vivid choreographic example of the use of the breath motif in a multiplicity of rhythms and forms is Doris Humphrey's *Water Study* (see Ex. 58). Performed without music, the composition begins with the undulating successional movement of fourteen dancers crouched on bent knees in different areas of the stage. At first, the flow of movement rippling through their bodies across the stage suggests the barely ruffled surface of a quiet sea. Gradually, the movement becomes more intense and the dancers, arching their backs, slide forward on their hands to "break" like waves upon a shore. Then, drawing themselves up and dividing to form two opposing lines on the far edges of the stage, they run and leap toward each other, colliding in the air and falling away like wind-swept waves in a stormy sea. The breath motif is maintained throughout the changing movements, and is particularly effective at the end when the "waves" subside as the dancers return to their crouching positions on the floor, and the successional movement ripples through their bodies once more.

STANDING AS FUNDAMENTAL EXPERIENCE

Gravity, momentum and inertia . . . affect all objects whether at rest or in motion . . . In maintaining a balanced position amidst contending forces, stresses are set up within a structure, the degree of which varies with the position, the weight, and the resistant properties of the several parts.[2]

The upright body centers its weight so that each part is aligned in balanced relationship. Steady, yet movable at all times, it resists forces that would dislodge it.

STANDING AS DANCE EXPERIENCE

Standing as dance experience appears to be still, yet its stillness has the potential of unlimited movement. Standing at the be-

[1] Humphrey, *The Art of Making Dances*, p. 107, 108.
[2] Todd, *The Thinking Body*, pp. 55-56.

Doris Humphrey in *Passacaglia*. Standing: the design is symmetrical; the feeling in the body is one of contained power.

ginning of a dance, or within the context of a dance, can be a gathering up of forces to be used moments later in acts of daring. Standing at the end of a dance can be a summing up of the composition's choreographic intention. The symmetry of standing need not be lifeless, but filled with the possibilities of releasing great reserves of energy. Apollonian in its perfected balancing, standing serves as a point of departure for the Dionysian fall.

CHANGE OF WEIGHT AS FUNDAMENTAL EXPERIENCE

As soon as we begin to move from the static standing position, we transfer our weight to one or the other foot. This is normally an automatic action, scarcely noticeable even to ourselves. Smoothness of muscular coordination facilitates the movement. When this is lacking, all shifting and propelling motions are executed with difficulty.

CHANGE OF WEIGHT AS DANCE EXPERIENCE

In the Humphrey movement, the sensation of bodily weight change is a vivid experience. Contact with the floor is a positive motion, not necessarily heavy in terms of accented sound but realistically firm. Although the body gives in to the ground (floor) as if pulled magnetically downward, it does this with a deliberate sense of its relationship to the earth. This action becomes a physical and emotional statement, a way of saying simply and unequivocally, "I am." To acknowledge reality was a basic premise of early modern dance. Being rooted meant having power; being rooted meant having identity. "The modern dancer," wrote Doris Humphrey, "must . . . establish his human relation to gravity and reality."[1]

WALKING AS FUNDAMENTAL EXPERIENCE

The first act of walking is to fall; the next is to catch the falling weight; and the third is the continuation of the other two acts in alternation and in rhythm, until the decision to reorganize the pattern of movement is made.[2]

Such is the basic action of the walk, which is described in more dramatic terms by the nineteenth-century philosopher, Arthur

[1] Humphrey, *My Approach to the Modern Dance*, p. 188.
[2] Todd, *The Thinking Body*, p. 207.

Schopenhauer: "It is clear that as our walking is admittedly nothing but a constantly prevented falling, so the life of our bodies is nothing but a constantly prevented dying . . ."[1] The walk, with its positive rhythmic pulse, is like the dynamic action existing in "The Arc Between Two Deaths," an act of affirmation. Doris Humphrey calls its rhythm, "a conscious joy in beat as the weight [is] changed."[2]

In the walk, forces of balance coordinate with forces of flow: arms swing oppositionally to legs, not only to save the moving form from falling, but to engineer the progression smoothly through space. Another manifestation of control is the succession of the body's traveling motion: first onto the heel of the extended foot, then over the instep and through the small muscles of the sole and toes of the foot. As a result of its steady rhythm, the walk has a fairly even reiterative "locomotive" beat.

WALKING AS DANCE EXPERIENCE

If we return to the premise that the Humphrey Technique is an exploration of movement as physiological-psychological experience, we recognize that the impulse behind the act of walking is the desire to move in a particular direction. Motivation, then, is the key to the walk as potential dance motion. With this in mind, the student dancer should approach the learning of the walk as ideal rhythmic coordination. The oppositional swing of arms and legs and the successional flow of body parts provide immediate understanding of the Humphrey principles of Oppositional Motion and Successional Flow. With all extraneous movements eliminated, the body functions in balanced unity.

Like the breath, the walk has infinite rhythmic resources. Changing the tempo from moderately slow to fast enlivens the action and changes the mood. Syncopation provides its own excitement. Half-time gives the walk gravity, nobility. Unevenness of step often adds a touch of comedy or grotesquerie. Vital evidence of the "will to live," the walk with its lift, drop, rebound, and carry-through is the foundation of almost every dance movement.

The first section of Doris Humphrey's *Drama of Motion* (1930), a three-part work without music, was an exquisite example of the choreographer's use of the rhythmic, dynamic, and design elements contained in the walk. Conceived as a processional, the dance

[1] Arthur Schopenhauer, *Counsels and Maxims*, p. 28, note.
[2] Humphrey, *The Art of Making Dances*, p. 105.

began with the appearance of three women standing statuesquely side by side on a platform upstage right. With lifted bodies and rounded gestures, they proceeded to step down and to walk slowly toward the audience. As they turned to cross the stage in frieze-like patterns of bending, scooping, and stretching, another trio of dancers appeared on the platform. They, too, proceeded downstage. In even order, two more groups advanced to follow as in a ritual the path made by the first trio, which by this time was moving upstage and exiting at a point directly opposite its entrance. Serene and formal in design, the *Drama of Motion* evoked the architectural splendor of the Erechtheum, the temple of Athena on the Acropolis where six draped goddess-like statues, known as the Caryatids, serve as columns to support a porch roof.

RUNNING AND LEAPING AS FUNDAMENTAL EXPERIENCE

Running is an exaggerated form of the act of walking. It is an intensification of the primary purpose: to reach a predetermined point in space. It can also represent most simply a burst of energy, leading the runner to nowhere in particular. In this sense, there is a conscious indulgence in the pleasure of the action itself.

As an exaggerated form of walking, running "streamlines" the body to a greater degree. With the body tilting forward and the feet flying, gravitational pull seems to be conquered. However, just as in the walk, it is still operative, equalizing down-thrust with up-thrust. The arms moving rapidly in conjunction with each advancing step would impede the action. Instead, supporting his arms loosely at his sides, the runner covers space like the wind. The momentum that he gathers "lines him up" perfectly for the leap.

Flexion of the ankles and knees becomes greater with the leap. The simultaneous "plié" of both joints acts as a coil which springs the runner into the air. Now the arms work more freely, coordinating when possible to lift the body off the ground. The leap is an exclamation point, a shout of the entire body.

RUNNING AND LEAPING AS DANCE EXPERIENCE

Subject to the limitations of studio or stage space, the run becomes a modified, though not necessarily less intensified, expression of the dancer's will. Actually, the performer is obliged to compress the energy involved in "normal" running into a more concentrated form. Compositionally, this compression amounts to "distortion," which is the choreographer's way of clarifying and heightening the impressions of what is being expressed. (Distortion is an element of composition in the Humphrey Technique.)

The natural buoyancy of the run may be emphasized in spurts which send the body off its course with falling motions that rhythmically break up the steady pace of advance. A plethora of variations might take place as spatial confinement dictates change of direction or uneven timing. Rich in its evocation of primary energy, the run yields treasures of rhythmic nuances and spatial explorations, the most exhilarating of these being the leap.

Ultimate expression of the moving organism, the leap gathers all bodily forces for the strenuous act of defying gravity midair. With momentum accumulating from a standing or running take-off, the leap gives the dancer the power to spin or assume various bodily conformations aloft. The battle with gravity must be rhythmically timed, however, for the landing has to be "cushioned". The body must proceed easily to the next movement if the leap is executed within the choreographic flow of a dance.

The leap, like the fall, must rebound from its own energies as it descends. When the leap is followed by a fall, as in *Water Study*, the landing rebound is bypassed; energy flows directly into the completed fall. The body then rises with delayed timing: its formerly centered weight has been redistributed over all parts of the organism, and the relaxed spread of the fall must be counteracted by gathering tension if recovery is to take place.

Brilliant and exciting, if skillfully maneuvered, the leap is the most daring statement of the human body. Leaping is a form of skywriting, evanescent but memorable to the last detail of its aerial configurations.

CONCLUSION

That the Humphrey Technique concentrates on these diverse natural actions and their ingredients is testimony to its founder's esthetic intention: "Deep in mind the aim is life revealed in art."[1] That these fundamental experiences and their potential dance elements—rhythm, dynamics, and design—are used in accordance

[1]Doris Humphrey Collection. Folder M-56.

with a philosophy that seeks to interrelate the physique and the psyche becomes increasingly apparent the more one studies the technique. The *dance experience,* which is the heart and soul of the Humphrey Technique, therefore encompasses more than the purely mechanical development or maintenance of body skills. It emerges as foremost evidence of Doris Humphrey's humanistic approach to movement, expressed in the following "declaration":

> I wish my dance to reflect some experience of my own in relationship to the outside world; to be based on reality illumined by imagination; to be organic rather than synthetic; to call forth a definite reaction from my audience; and to make its contribution toward the drama of life.[1]

[1] Humphrey, *"My Approach to the Modern Dance,"* pp. 188-189.

PART TWO

THE TECHNIQUE AS PRACTICE

To dance well, technical mastery of the
body is the first prerequisite.
  Doris Humphrey, *My Approach to the Modern Dance*

Introduction

All the exercises and studies in Part Two derive their impetus and form—spatial, rhythmic, and dynamic—from the principles discussed in Part One. It is therefore necessary that the philosophical and theoretical background of the Humphrey Technique remains firmly fixed in the teachers' and students' minds when approaching "The Technique as Practice."

An abundance of material in each of the following chapters deals with fundamental aspects of the movement vocabulary. This makes it possible for the teacher to select those exercises which best meet the needs of the students on a progressive basis. Consistent practice will develop familiarity with and competence in the movement style; technical skills should increase steadily.

The four chapters of Part Two constitute, in sequence, the curriculum of a single lesson: center work, floor work, barre work, and spatial sequences. Within each section, elementary exercises progress to complex studies, providing graded material commensurate with the students' growing abilities to absorb and express the characteristics of the technique.

Many of the original movements created by Doris Humphrey for classroom use and lecture-demonstrations are analyzed and described in detail. Intermingled with these are exercises and studies which I have developed as a teacher of Humphrey principles.

Studying and performing the movements described in Chapters 3-6 will, I hope, provide the reader-dancer with the exciting experience of learning a way of moving which has been described by its creator as "light, radiance, wholeness (clarity, intensity, unity of action)."[1]

TERMINOLOGY

Some of the terms employed by Doris Humphrey in her approach to dance training will be used from time to time in the instructions. Listed alphabetically, they are:

Design
Dynamics
Isolation
Phrasing
Rebound
Rhythm
Successional
Tension and Relaxation
Wholeness

Design: "Every movement made by a human being . . . has a design in space. . . ."[2] References throughout the exercises to abstract forms, such as circles, figure eights, angles, convex and concave curvatures seen and experienced as either planal or three-dimensional movement, emphasize the conscious use of design as a choreographic ingredient in the Humphrey style.

Dynamics: In dance, movement expressive of "variations in tempo and tension."[3] Action subject to changing forces of momentum or, by contrast, inertia.

Isolation: The separate use of a single part (or related parts) of the body for the purposes of freeing or strengthening those parts independently. For example: working one foot at a time separately (or both together) to develop muscular proficiency in the arches, toes, and ankles.

[1] Doris Humphrey Collection. Folder M-91.
[2] Humphrey, *The Art of Making Dances*, p. 46.
[3] Humphrey, *The Art of Making Dances*, p. 47.

Phrasing: The grouping of movements in a sequence which emphasizes movement flow in terms of rhythm, design, and quality (time, space, and dynamics). Whether she used music as her accompaniment or presented her dances in silence, Doris Humphrey conceived her dance movements in rhythmic-dynamic sequences. To quote the choreographer: ". . . every movement phrase of this repertory [Limón Dance Company performances, London, 1957] is consciously colored by dynamic shifts consonant with the theme. . . ."[1]

Rebound: For complete analysis, see Chapter 2, p. 20.

Rhythm: Called by Doris Humphrey "the great organizer."[2] Rhythmic training in the Humphrey tradition aims to develop awareness through kinetic response to simple and complex rhythms independent of musical reference. It is also used in conjunction with analysis of and response to music.

Successional: In the Humphrey vocabulary of movement analysis, this has two similar but not identical connotations. The first, which forms part of a trilogy of Natural Body Designs[3] with Opposition and Unison movement, refers to movements which operate progressively through space, such as the continuous action involved in walking or running, or a choreographed progression of accents from one dancer to another. The second refers to the successional flow of energy *within* the body in a given direction (see description of Breathing as Dance Experience, Chapter 2, p. 21. When describing Successional Flow, we shall differentiate thusly: in succession (first meaning); successional motion (second meaning).

Tension and Relaxation: Elements present in all motion, "natural motion meaning using the body as all organic things move: up or out with effort, down or in without effort. In the absence of effort or tension there is relaxation—the negative opposite to tension."[4] Tension and Relaxation are the basic ingredients of Humphrey-style movements. Tension maintains the body's balance. Relaxation incurs Falling. The Rebound (Recovery) introduces tension again by gradually restoring balance. As equilibrium is being regained, there is the transitory stage of Suspension.

---

[1] "Doris Humphrey Answers the Critics," *Dance and Dancers* (London: March 1959).
[2] Humphrey, *The Art of Making Dances*, p. 104.
[3] Doris Humphrey Collection. Folder M-85.
[4] Doris Humphrey Collection. Folder M-58.

Wholeness: Completely synchronized rhythmic coordination in a given assignment. A Swing, for instance, involves action of the torso, head, legs, and feet in conjunction with the arms, which appear to be the principle agents in performing the movement. Wholeness, as integrated movement, is the most typical dance characteristic of the Humphrey style.

Other Teaching Terms Employed

Parallel: Standing position in which the legs facing front are lined up directly beneath the hip joints. The distance between the feet is approximately 1 ½" to 2", depending on the body's proportions.

Turn-Out: The placement of the leg (legs) in outward rotation from the hip joint. The modern dance "turn-out" is moderate compared to that of classic ballet.

Side-Back: A twisting motion of the torso from the waist, approximately 1/8 turn toward either side, with a backward pull or tilt.

Concave, Convex: Two views of the same movement. When cited as description, for example, "back is convex," the intention is to induce a sensation of a front *overcurve* as the principal attribute of that particular bodily position (and design) in space. Such a description is an attempt to encourage the student to develop a sense of "volume" within the space enclosed by the movement.

Lunge: A full-length step forward or sideways on one leg, bending the knee while keeping the heel on the floor. The stationary leg is fully stretched (knee may be straight or slightly bent) with the foot or toes still on the floor.

Off-Balance: A term describing the act of falling. In the Humphrey style, an extreme off-balance movement is possible by virtue of balancing controls which are developed through the technique.

FORMAT OF THE DESCRIPTIVE MATERIAL

It was Doris Humphrey's custom when teaching or directing to acquaint her students and dancers first with the esthetic concept behind a series of movements before analyzing the action itself. Such a method yielded rich results. It immediately established a mutually creative working relationship between the teacher-director and the interpreters of her choreographic ideas.

Following this pattern of presentation, I have described the choreographic intentions behind most of the exercises, studies, and dance sequences in Part Two before explaining the physical procedures. Through this method it is hoped that today's teachers, directors, and students will discover, as we did, the inspirational benefits of creative collaboration in the evolution of a choreographic concept.

MOVEMENTS OF ARMS, HEAD, AND HANDS

In the Humphrey style, arms move from the torso, not solely from the shoulder joint. The entire upper body is involved in the action. A stretching of the arms upward is a pull or lift from the waist. A stretching of the arms backward is likewise a motion involving the back, chest, and stomach muscles. There is also a corresponding action in the pelvis and the legs; as we have indicated in our explanation of *Wholeness*, most Humphrey-style movements are accomplished through rhythmic coordination of various parts of the body. The exceptions are exercises in Isolation and those sequences which are "stylized" for particular choreographic reasons: a period flavor, satire, or dramatic emphasis. In such cases, the body movement is formalized, or, as Doris Humphrey would say, "intensified and distorted" from the natural for purposes of exaggeration.

Because the arms and the spine move conjunctively, the head is part of the process, and any lift of the arms requires a corresponding reaction in the neck and head. In the same way, the head must participate in motions which are downward or falling. When falling backward or sideways, the head does not drop "off," hanging from the neck, but tilts with the body in a specific direction akin to that of the arm movements. For example, if the dancer is executing overdrops (see Exercises 18-19), the head drops with the torso to the side, curving naturally as the arms open. The face is upturned and the eyes are focused upward. There should be no strain in the neck.

The hands, too, are part of the total action. They are never indifferently used. Alive to every nuance of feeling, they reflect the dancer's moods. One of the most typical Humphrey hand statements is a lifted arm gesture in which the palm is facing out, the wrist pressing forward slightly, and the fingers extended upward without strain. Such a gesture is directed to the world at large. Used in *Passacaglia,* Doris Humphrey's monumental work to Johann Sebastian Bach's *Passacaglia and Fugue in C Minor,* it becomes a statement of faith in man's power to surmount all obstacles.

MUSICAL ACCOMPANIMENT AND CONTINUITY

Assuming that music is used as accompaniment for the subsequent exercises, it is suggested that those movements which are built on the same dynamic principles—successional motion, isolations, swings, and so forth—be performed in "clusters," for which the music could conceivably supply a similarly evolving continuity. Such an accompaniment would assist the dancer in maintaining the pace and quality of the movement while working on the skills involved. As soon as the individual exercises are mastered rhythmically and technically, the "clustering" process will reveal further benefits: introducing improvisation as a method of linking movements; discovering continuity of action through contrast or flow.

It is also suggested that some of the movements be practiced first without music. This enables the student to concentrate on the changing speeds of the fall/recovery motions without having to conform to a musical beat or phrase. Accordingly, the student becomes aware of the gradations within the dynamics of the movement.

Please note that all tempo markings are metronomically indicated. The purpose is to provide timing references for the teacher and the accompanist. When there is no accompaniment, the teacher's personal feeling for movement phrasing should be the guide. Tempo is a matter of temperament; slight variations from the suggested markings are acceptable. The metronome itself should never be used for accompaniment inasmuch as the ticking is mechanical and, therefore, contrary to all natural body impulses.

COUNTING PATTERNS

Counting in the more conventional musical patterns—2/4, 3/4, 4/4, and 6/8 time—is used in the early sections of Part Two to facilitate learning the movement sequences. As phrases become more complex and the exercises are expanded, counting patterns become less conventional, and uneven rhythmic sequences are introduced.

BODY PLACEMENT

Technical advances in American modern dance since the time of pioneer exploration have made today's teachers conscious of the fact that correct body placement is a scientifically sound means of realizing the body's fullest dance potential. Correct alignment is, therefore, of utmost importance within the context of a given technique.

Since the Humphrey Technique is basically kinetic, correct alignment is best taught through the act of moving, rather than as static experience. From the beginning of the training, it is necessary to cultivate the pupils' awareness of the body's balancing needs. Once students begin to work with and counteract gravitational pull through the principles of Fall and Recovery, they will be obliged to draw upon their own physical resources; in doing so, they should be trained to feel (and see, if a mirror is used) whether they are correctly aligned *as they move.* The educated eye of the teacher should be the final judge, for it is his or her responsibility to recognize that "the human being is a composite of balanced forces."[1]

[1]Todd, *The Thinking Body,* p. 7.

Chapter 3
CENTER WORK

INTRODUCTION

Beginning with very simple movements, the technique develops into complexly organized coordinations. The aims of the following preliminary exercises (1-7) are to speed up circulatory flow in all parts of the body through rhythmic action and breath intake, and to introduce the use of successional movement in various directions based on Fall/Recovery principles.

SUCCESSIONS

1. SUCCESSIONAL MOVEMENT: Vertical

An exercise designed to establish a sense of movement-flow rising and falling perpendicularly through the body. The first phrase is preparatory in that the breath is expelled and the body relaxes; with a fresh intake of breath, energy is renewed and the body lifts successionally.

Count: Four phrases of 4 beats each. All successional movements are initiated by the breath.

Tempo: 48 (Moderately slow) *Music Quality:* Sustained, flowing.

Starting Position: Feet parallel, about 2″ apart. Body facing front, arms relaxed at sides, knees straight. Focus forward.

Phrase 1: (Cts 1- 4) With gradual exhalation of breath, the body drops over with a sinking motion toward the floor, letting the movement increase in speed until the knees are well bent and the fingers lightly touch the floor. The body is now rounded over at half height; breath is completely expelled.

Phrase 2: (Cts 1- 4)   Four soft bounces in the drop-over position, arms still falling naturally, knees taking the rhythmic impulse. Breathing is natural.

Phrase 3: With gradual intake of breath, begin the recovery successionally by tilting the knees downward which lifts the hips forward, back still rounded (Cts 1-2). As the successional motion rises through the torso the movement comes to a peak with the back arching slightly (Ct 3), then the head drops back, eyes looking up (Ct 4).

Phrase 4: Four soft bounces in the knees while in the arched position (Cts 1-4). Breathing is natural.

Suggested Repetition: A minimum of 4 times.

Note: Be sure that the upward successional movement through the hips is well articulated, i.e., the hips swing under, propelled by the thigh muscles, and remain forward in alignment under the shoulders as the torso motion continues, followed by the bounces.

1. SUCCESSIONAL MOVEMENT: Vertical

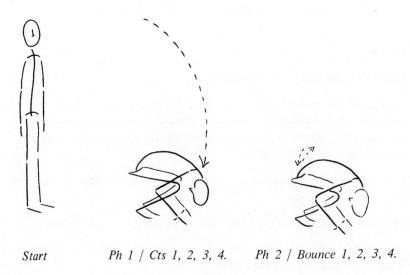

Start   *Ph 1 / Cts 1, 2, 3, 4.*   *Ph 2 / Bounce 1, 2, 3, 4.*

Ph 1 / Cts 1, 2 . . . . .3, 4.   *Ph 2 / Bounce 1, 2, 3, 4.*

Variation: *Double-time motion.*

Count: Two phrases of 4 beats each.

Tempo and *Music Quality:* Same as above.

Starting Position: The arched position reached in Phrase 4 above.

Phrase 1: Breath is inhaled (Ct 1), then exhaled (Ct 2) as the body falls with increasing speed. The bounces now occur on Cts 3-4.

Phrase 2: The recovery begins as breath is inhaled with body lift (Cts 1-2), then exhaled with arched bounces (Cts 3-4).

2. SUCCESSIONAL MOVEMENT: Sideways

Sideways flow of movement through the body and arm rising in a convex curve and descending in a concave curve.

Count: Four phrases of 3 beats each (right and left).

Tempo: 48 (Moderately slow)   *Music Quality:* Sustained, flowing.

Starting Position: Feet parallel, about 1½" to 2" apart. Body facing front, arms relaxed at sides, knees relaxed.

Phrase 1: *Ascent.* With intake of breath, successional movement starts through the entire right side of the body: slight impulse in the knees as the R arm begins lifting at the elbow (Ct 1), continues rising in expanding curve (Ct 2) as breath "travels" sideways through the torso into the arm. Body is now bending left as the arm pulls upward stretching through the wrist and hand with the fingers fully unfolded by Ct 3. Head has dropped to the left as well, with the face looking sideways up toward the right; the L arm, though inactive, curves outward slightly at the elbow and wrist. By the end of Ct 3, R arm is fully stretched and body has slowly pulled up as well on the right side, without straightening completely.

Phrase 2: Descent. Arm now reverses direction, pulling down with elbow, palm facing out (Ct 1), then pressing wrist as body bends to right (Ct 2), and finishes with the fingers softly pressing downward (Ct 3). Head and eyes follow the movement sideways-down. Knees have bent accordingly, allowing the movement to be articulated throughout the entire body, as the breath is slowly exhaled. Here, too, the L arm, though inactive, remains slightly curved outward at the elbow and wrist.

Phrases 3 and 4: Repeat on the left side.

Suggested Repetition: 3 times.

Variation: Broken descent. On the descent to the right, instead of bringing the arm down with a smooth pressing motion of the elbow bending sideways-out, bend the elbow sharply inward across the torso in a sudden falling movement (Ct 4). The wrist and hand remain in a straight line pointing outward, but the body and head correspondingly bend sideways towards the arm. On Cts 5-6, a secondary drop takes place, in which the hand falls across the torso and the forearm swings inward and down returning to its original position alongside the body. Torso and head bend briefly in the other direction and then recover. A fresh impulse in the knees to the right starts the sideways succession again on the same side (Cts 1-2-3).

Repeat to the left. Then alternate, allowing the hips and body to swing freely within the rhythmic form of the movement.

2. SUCCESSIONAL MOVEMENT: Sideways

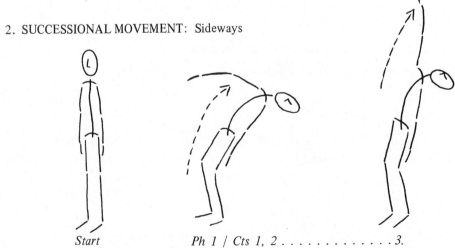

Start   *Ph 1 / Cts 1, 2 . . . . 3.*

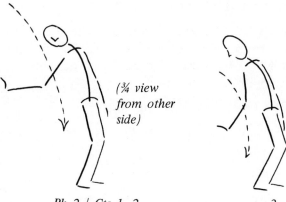

Ph 2 / Cts 1, 2 . . . . *3.*

Variation: Broken Descent

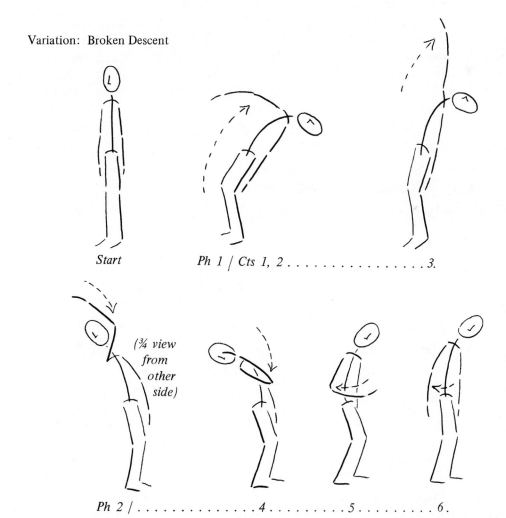

Start   *Ph 1 / Cts 1, 2* . . . . *3.*

Ph 2 / . . . . *4* . . . . *5* . . . . *6.*

(¾ view from other side)

(¾ view from other side)

3. SIDEWAYS SUCCESSION WITH DROP AND GRAVITATIONAL PULL

Increasing the energy of the Sideways Succession into an intensified pull, the dancer now reaches so far up that a fall is inevitable. The fall, taking the form of a sideways lunge, is followed by a weighted pull back to center, from which the movement recommences with the other arm.

Count: Two phrases of 8 beats each (right and left).

Tempo: 50 (Moderately slow) *Music Quality:* Strong impulses (accents) at the beginning of the phrase.

Starting Position: Feet parallel, about 2" apart.

Phrase 1: Sideways succession (as above) with R arm pulling body tautly up-ward to a point of suspension by Ct 4. On Ct 5, with breath exhalation, body drops sharply to the right, catching the weight in a lunge onto the R foot about 2½' to the side, knee well bent, heel on the floor. R arm has dropped to the side as well. Cts 6-8, with a heavy sense of gravitational pull, draw the R leg slowly back to parallel position, the body (still low, fingers almost touching floor) also drawing back and gradually changing the side-drop of the torso into a front over-drop by the count of 8.

Phrase 2: Sideways succession with the L arm rising (as above) and the lunge-drop on the L leg with breath exhalation, etc. (Cts 1-8).

3. SIDEWAYS SUCCESSION WITH DROP AND GRAVITATIONAL PULL

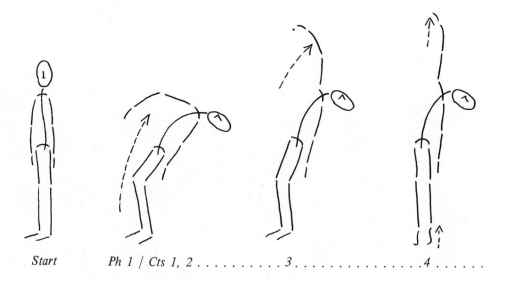

Start   *Ph 1 / Cts 1, 2* . . . . *3* . . . . *4* . . . . . .

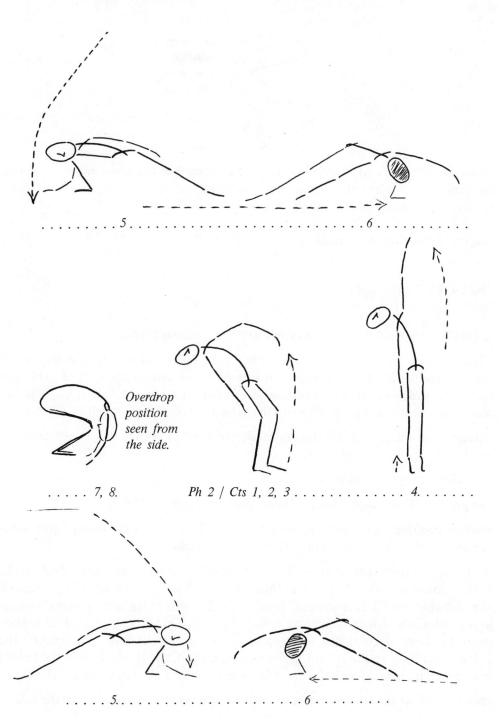

. . . . 5 . . . . 6 . . . .

*Overdrop
position
seen from
the side.*

. . . . . 7, 8.   *Ph 2 / Cts 1, 2, 3* . . . . 4 . . . . . .

. . . . . . 5 . . . . 6 . . . .

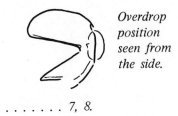

*Overdrop
position
seen from
the side.*

. . . . 7, 8.

Note: On the point of suspension (Ct 4), the stretch of the body involves the legs and feet to the degree that knees are fully stretched and feet are in relevé (heels up, weight balanced on the balls of the feet).

Suggested Repetition: A minimum of 3 times.

CHANGES OF WEIGHT

4. CHANGE OF WEIGHT WITH FALLING MOTION: Walking Version

Remembering that the walk is a progression in a given direction, it is important that the feeling in the body is one of intention and anticipation. The lift in the torso and head is alive with purpose as the dancer takes the first step. The fall comes as a result of losing balance (figuratively) and also of expelling the breath.

Count: Two phrases of 4 beats each. Starting with the R foot, a five-step movement on beats 1, 2, 3, "and," 4.

Direction: Forward and back.

Tempo: 48 (Moderately slow)   *Music Quality:* Strong, flowing.

Starting Position: Feet parallel, about 1 ½" to 2" apart. Body facing front, arms relaxed at sides. Knees straight without undue tension.

Phrase 1: Starting with R foot, body breath-filled, lifted torso, step: R, L, R, L, R (full count is 1-4). On Cts 1-2, the body remains lifted as it advances, focus of eyes forward; on Ct 3, a sense of gravitational pull is being felt as though one is losing balance and is in danger of falling forward. On Ct "and" (the double-time step), the body starts falling forward in an over-curve, catching its weight on the L foot, and then on the R foot (knee well bent) on Ct 4, at which time the breath is completely exhaled and the arms fall naturally with the body toward the floor.

Phrase 2: Now the movement is reversed in space. In recovering from the falling motion, step backward L, R (Cts 1-2), smoothly pulling upward through the body successively (knees, hips, torso, neck, head) with the full height achieved by Ct 2. Now the gravitational pull is backward, the breath is inhaled, and the arms curve outward with a slight sense of suspension. The same sense of falling begins to take over as the dancer steps L (Ct 3), R (Ct "and"), then falls side-back[1] on the L leg (Ct 4) with L leg turned out at a 45-degree angle, the knee bent. R knee is also bent, but facing front. Breath is completely exhaled. Head and shoulders have relaxed in a side-back curve of body, with face tilted upward. Throughout the backward walk, arms are held in soft convex curves from shoulders to wrists, somewhat formalizing the walk. On the side-back fall, the arms relax naturally alongside the body.

Suggested Repetition: A minimum of 4 times (2 phrases each time).

Repeat, starting with the L foot.

4. CHANGE OF WEIGHT WITH FALLING MOTION: Walking Version

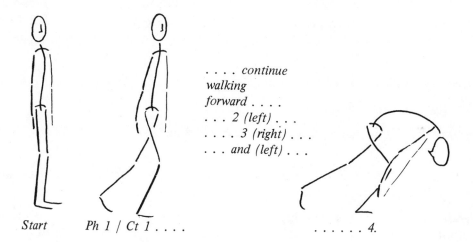

. . . . *continue*
walking
forward . . . .
. . . 2 (left) . . .
. . . . 3 (right) . . .
. . . and (left) . . .

Start   *Ph 1 / Ct 1 . . . .*   *. . . . . . 4.*

---

[1] See definition of "side-back", p. 34.

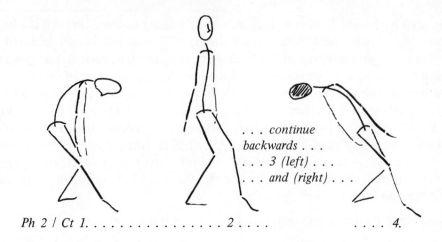

... continue
backwards ...
... 3 (left) ...
... and (right) ...

Ph 2 / Ct 1. . . . . 2 . . . .   *. . . . 4.*

5. CHANGE OF WEIGHT WITH FALLING MOTION: Single Step

A sense of being unable to remain in balance dominates the first action of this movement, which results in a weighted stepping forward on one leg as though pulled to the ground. Not giving in to gravity altogether, the dancer rebounds[1] to standing, but is subsequently pulled backward so that a partial fall to the side-back takes place (on the same leg). A forward and backward arching motion of the body.

Count: One phrase of 4 beats.

Direction: Forward and back.

Tempo: 42 (Slow and well-accented on beats 2 and 4)   *Music Quality:* Lyrical, yet emphatic.

Starting Position: Weight on R foot, L foot at ease. Face front, torso lifted, arms hanging naturally downward.

Phrase: Inhale breath with body pulled upward (Ct 1); then exhale and drop over L foot with body falling forward, leg turned out at 45-degree angle to stabilize weight (Ct 2). Recover with inhalation in successional lift through torso, neck, and head, while arms swell slightly to the side in convex curves (Ct 3). Drop backward onto L foot (similar angle of turn-out), letting the body fall side-back to the left (as in Ex. 4) with exhalation of breath, arms falling to sides in natural release of elbows toward gravity (Ct 4). There is a strong rhythmic pulse throughout the movement, which is initiated by the inhalation and exhalation of the breath.

[1] See definition of "rebound," p. 20.

Suggested Repetition: A minimum of 8 times.

Repeat, starting on the L foot and immediately drop over R foot.

5. CHANGE OF WEIGHT WITH FALLING MOTION: Single Step

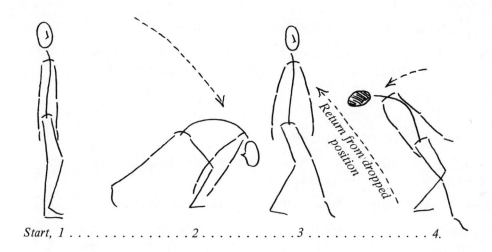

Start, 1 . . . . *2* . . . . *3* . . . . *4.*

ISOLATIONS

Isolation is the use of a single body part for the purposes of freeing and strengthening that part independently.

6. SHOULDER ROLL

Count: One circular movement of 4 beats.

Tempo: 48 (Moderately slow)   *Music Quality:* Slow, resonant.

Starting Position: Feet parallel. Body facing front, arms relaxed at sides, knees straight.

Phrase: Both shoulders roll forward, upward, then backward and down (Cts 1-4). The head remains in position without tension. Repeat several times.

Repeat, as above, reversing direction.

7. HEAD ROLL

Count, Tempo, and *Starting Position:* Same as above.

Phrase: Head tilts, dropping to the right, then rolls across the chest to the left and continues backward with dropping motion, completing the circle (Cts 1-4).

Repeat for a total of 2 times; then reverse direction.

8. FEET

Count, Tempo, and *Starting Position:* Same as above.

Phrase: Stretching the arch, press forward over the ball of each foot by lifting the heel forcibly. Release and return to heel, placing weight on foot.

Repeat several times.

9. FORWARD CIRCLES OF THE ARMS

Count: Begin with 4 beats. Phrases develop with changing emphasis and timing as the movements are further explored.

Tempo: 48 (Moderately slow)   *Music Quality:* Same as above.

Starting Position: Feet parallel. Body facing front, arms relaxed at sides, knees straight, shoulders at ease, face lifted slightly in anticipation of motion.

Phrase 1: R arm lifts forward from the shoulder (which remains quiet throughout the following movements) with elbow and wrist slightly curved, palm facing down (Ct 1). The body is lifted slightly from the waist. On Ct 2, the arm has reached the zenith of the circle and is above the shoulder with the fingers pointing upward. On Ct 3, the arm turns outward and starts the descent toward the back. On Ct 4, the arm returns to place, releasing the energy.

Repeat with L arm.

Total repeat of Phrase 1.

Phrase 2: The same action double time. With similar repeat.

Note: The breath has been coordinated throughout these movements: inhalation on lift of arm, exhalation on descent.

Note: Since all the above "isolated" exercises are done in approximately the same tempo, it is suggested that the teacher incorporate them all into a continuous sequence, a method which will be increasingly used as the dancers become more efficient in the separate movements.

6-9. SHOULDER ROLL, HEAD ROLL, FEET, FORWARD CIRCLE OF THE ARMS

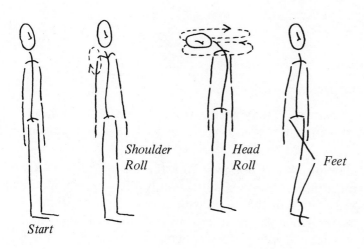

Shoulder Roll   *Head Roll*   *Feet*

Start

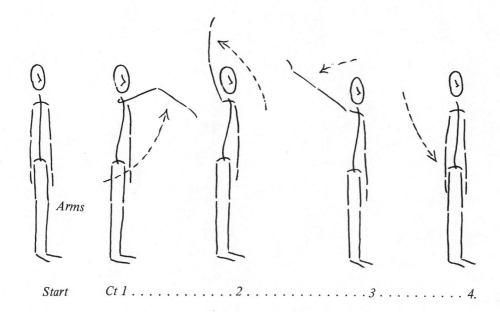

Arms

Start   Ct 1 . . . . 2 . . . . 3 . . . . 4.

BASIC STRETCHES

Body bends in various directions emphasizing tension and relaxation with coordinated arm and head movements.

10. WAIST

Count: A movement, and a recovery of 4 beats each.

Tempo: 58   *Music Quality:* Well-accented.

Starting Position: Feet parallel. Body facing front, L arm over the head, bent sharply at the elbow, forearm resting on top of the head. R arm hangs alongside the body.

Phrase: Bending to the right, 4 soft bounces from the waist (Cts 1-4). Rebound from Ct 4 with R arm lifting as L arm simultaneously lifts, stretching overhead (Cts 5-6). On the upward stretch, the body assumes a straight position. An exchange now takes place in which the R arm drops over the head and the L arm falls alongside the body with a subsequent waist bend to the left (Cts 7-8). Breath is inhaled as the transition begins and exhaled at the end, with natural breathing on the bounces.

Suggested Repetition: A minimum of 2 times on each side.

10. WAIST

Waist: Start   Bounce 1, 2, 3, 4, . . . 5, 6 . . . 7, 8.

11. UPPER LEG

Count and *Tempo:* Same as above.

Starting Position: Legs widely apart, turned out at a 45-degree angle with weight evenly divided.   Fingers placed on front surface of hipbones; thumbs on rear surface.

Phrase: Shift weight to R leg, bending R knee over foot in 4 emphatic rebounding movements to stretch the R thigh (Cts 1-4, with rebounds on "and"). On Ct 4-"and", straighten legs passing through center position to shift weight to L leg, and repeat the 4-count stretch.

Repeat, using both arms in a diagonal stretch overhead on same side as knee bend, with torso inclined in diagonal line. This adds body weight to the stretch.

Transition from combined diagonal stretch (leg, arms, torso): Drop the body across the pelvis from right to left, swinging downward with relaxed arms to rise to the other side. Diagonal position is now assumed on the left. Duration of the transition is 4 beats (Cts 5-8).

Repeat on left, with reverse transition.

11. UPPER LEG

Leg: Start   *Stretch 1* . . . . *and* . . . .

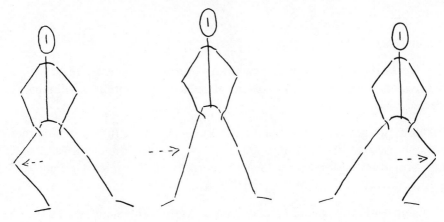

. . . 2 . . repeat 3 and 4 . . . and . . . . 1 . . . repeat and 2
and 3 and 4.

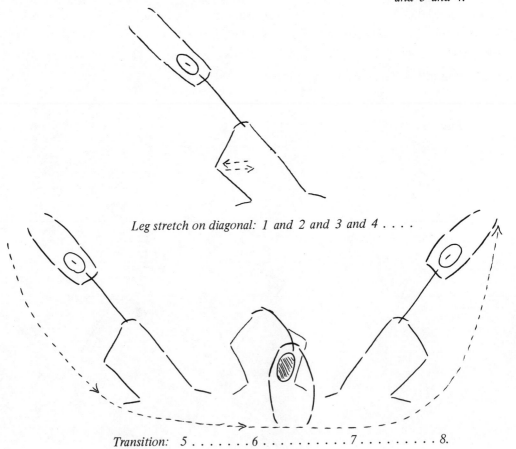

Leg stretch on diagonal: 1 and 2 and 3 and 4 . . . .

Transition: 5 . . . . 6 . . . . 7 . . . . 8.

12. BODY BENDS

Count: In 8s.

Tempo and *Music Quality:* Same as above.

Starting Position: As above, wide stance, legs parallel. Arms relaxed at sides.

Phrase: Fall forward and down with rounded back for relaxed stretch, fingers touching the floor. Eight soft bounces with legs straight (Cts 1-8). Recover, bringing body and arms up successively in forward curves (elbows and wrists lifting, palms facing down) to overhead (Cts 1-4). At peak of lift on Ct 4, heels come off the floor and the body's weight rests briefly on the balls of the feet; as the heels descend, they rotate inward allowing the legs to be turned out at a 45-degree angle. The arms are opening out circularly to the back and will come to rest with hands on hips, while the torso and head start to fall backward (Cts 5-8) from the high vertical position (do not let head drop back completely). The knees bend and the body's weight is supported in the thighs. In the final "falling" position, the back is arched with the hips lifted forward. Holding backward stretch with hips lifted, bounce softly (Cts 1-8). Reverse direction, scooping the arms backward in a circle until the body is again stretched upward, arms overhead (Cts 1-4). The heels are once again raised in transition on Ct 4. As the body falls forward and downward, the heels shift to parallel again, and the arms drop successionally in front—elbows, wrists, (palms facing in), hands—with the head and body following (Cts 5-8).

Repeat several times, coordinating the breath.

Note: This exercise may be done in 4 counts rather than 8 as the body becomes more flexible.

12. BODY BENDS

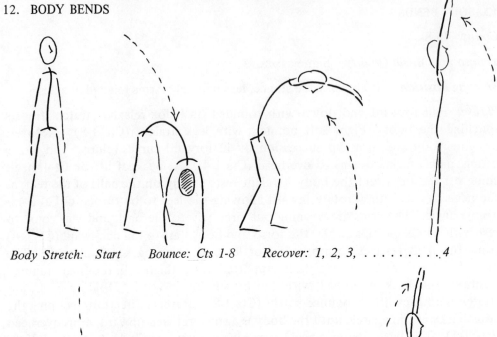

Body Stretch: Start Bounce: Cts 1-8 Recover: 1, 2, 3, ...4

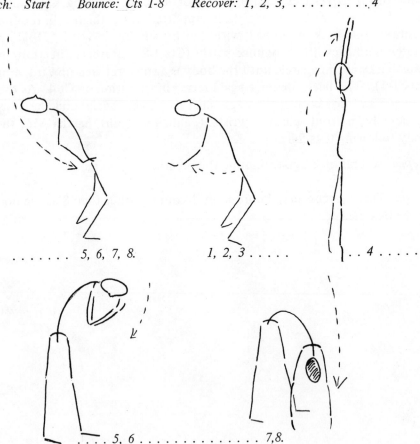

. . . . 5, 6, 7, 8.   1, 2, 3 . . . . 4 . . . . .

. . . . 5, 6 . . . . 7,8.

EXERCISE-STUDY

13. FAST WARM-UP

Continuously rapid footwork involving the body as a whole in differentiated motions. A necessary means of oxygenating the muscles.

Tempo: 132 (Fast) *Music Quality:* Lively, sharply accented.

Starting Position: Body facing front. Weight on L leg, R knee flexed forward, toes of R foot touching the floor lightly. Hands behind the back, resting against the spine, waist high.

Action begins with quick shiftings of weight in prance-like movement, knees lifting forward (Cts 1-3). On Ct 4, hop on the R foot, then repeat the movement starting with the L foot. Shoulders remain in place without stiffness.

Repeat several times.

Change to sideways kicking motions, knee of extended leg straight and facing front, toes pointed. Body is still facing front. Arms are extended sideways, shoulder height. Rhythm remains the same with alternate foot hopping on Ct 4.

Repeat several times.

Change to a steady 8-Count sideways kick (no hops). Arms start circling down sideways with wrists pressing, then cross in front of the body. With elbows and wrists initiating the movement, they circle upward in front of the body and head, returning to the side (Cts 1-8).

Repeat several times.

Turn one-eighth to the right, a diagonal position facing the downstage-right corner of the room. Now arms are held in opposition to the legs—left arm forward balances right forward-kicking leg—and the torso remains upright without stiffness. Count in 8s, then change without pause to face the downstage-left corner of the room with corresponding oppositional change of arms.

Repeat several times.

Continuing, march in place, facing front, knees sharply bent, hands on hips, and torso erect. Toes are pointed down. Count in 8s.

Repeat march with directional changes (forward and back, turning, etc.).

Final Sequence: Achilles Tendon Stretch. From parallel position, facing front, step forward on R foot into a semi-lunge (legs still in parallel relationship) and bend R knee over foot (heel on floor); the back leg is stretched straight but the heel is slightly raised. With most of the weight on forward foot, tilt body in slanted line, hands on hips, wrists dropped, shoulders facing front. Pushing forward into R thigh, bounce 8 times to stretch the Achilles tendon of the L leg. Jump-Change to repeat the movement on the other leg. Break the counts of the bouncing down to 6s, then 4s, then 2s, as you repeat the motion in rapid succession. Finally, change continuously, trying to press the heel of the back foot to the floor each time. Swing the arms in opposition as you change, as if running in place.

Note: Most of these movements may also be performed turning.

13.   FAST WARM-UP

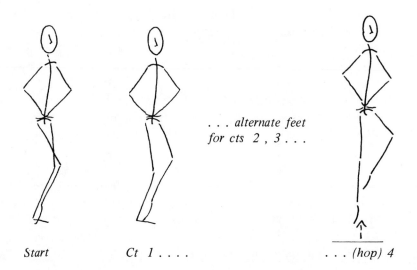

*. . . alternate feet
for cts 2 , 3 . . .*

Start   *Ct 1 . . . .*   *. . . (hop) 4*

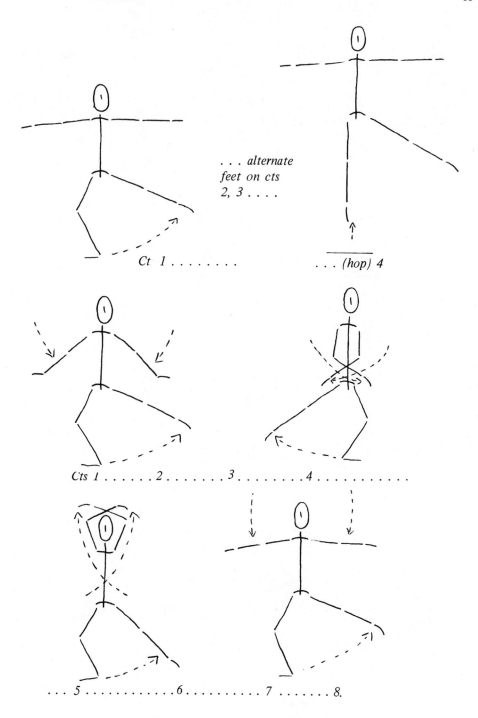

. . . alternate feet on cts 2, 3 . . . .

Ct 1 . . . .

. . . (hop) 4

Cts 1 . . . . . . 2 . . . . 3 . . . . 4 . . . .

. . . 5 . . . . 6 . . . . 7 . . . . . . 8.

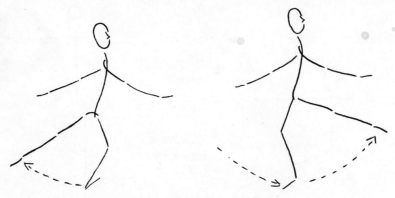

Diagonal kick: Cts 1-8; on both sides

March: Cts 1-8

Achilles tendon stretch . . . .

. . . with continuous change of feet and arms in opposition

EXTENDED PATTERNS: Swings

Full body swings are vividly expressive of the Humphrey Fall and Recovery principles. Coordinating when possible with the breath rhythms of inhalation and exhalation, the swing incorporates the fall, its rebound, and subsequent suspension. Swings are performed in a variety of directions: forward and backward, side to side, arms crossing and opening in coordination with lifting and dropping motions of the body, spiraling sequences, and so on. They are also used in conjunction with other falling-recovering movements. The pervading feeling is a sense of freedom combined with power.

The swing demands stability in the legs and torso at all times; the surge of movement requires firm positioning, especially when the body's weight is supported by one leg. In this instance, there must be adequate tension in the upper body to counteract the pull of an off-balance suspension.

It is important to recognize and emphasize the changing momentum of the swing as it accelerates and decelerates according to the force of gravitational pull, increasing with downward thrust and decreasing with recovery. It is also important to "release" the energies in the body so that the action of the swing is completely natural. In teaching the Humphrey Technique, the teacher often repeats, "Let go," when the student seems reticent in allowing the swing to take the body into off-balance positions.

Since the swing initiates a falling motion, it is apparent that the Dionysian principle of abandonment is at work here, particularly when the swinging motion encompasses the entire body. Relaxing the muscles of the neck, torso, and arms makes possible the smooth articulation of the entire body. The knees coordinate by bending with the impulse of the swing.

14. UP AND FORWARD, DOWN AND BACK

Count: Two-swing phrase of 6 beats.

Tempo: 104   *Music Quality:* Vibrant, sustained.

Starting Position: Feet parallel. Body facing front, arms lifted backward and upward in convex curves, elbows and wrists pulling, chin slightly dropped as head looks down, legs straight without stiffness.

Phrase: Swing downward and forward with both arms, curving the body over with the motion. Elbows reverse direction from curving backward convexly to lifting forward through elbows and wrists until arms are overhead in a high forward stretch (Cts 1-3). Arms are lifted and dropped "successionally". In the backward swing, drop the body well forward again as the arms descend, elbows pulling downward, palms facing the body at first and then remaining upturned as they pass alongside the body through the lowest point of the swing (Cts 4-6). Knees have bent and stretched with the swinging motions, and heels have pulled up slightly from the ground on Cts 3 and 6 as the body achieves the peak positions. The entire body is also moving in successional flow (see Exercise 1).

Repeat several times, using the breath in coordination with the swing.

Variation I: *Twist and Rebound.* Total of 15 Cts (count 1-2-3, 2-2-3, etc.). Using the Phrase above as a basic pattern for the first 6 Cts, continue the swinging motion. When arms swing upward again coming to a full overhead stretch (Cts 3-2-3), twist the body in an arch sideways to the right, the head dropping left and the face looking up. At the same time, with the feet wide apart and parallel, the R foot and knee facing front, extend the R leg to the right, and let the weight fall partially on it, still lifting sideways and upward through the torso (Ct 4). The arms, opening sideways to shoulder height, have made the quarter-turn with the body and are curved concavely. Rebound on Cts (4)-2-3-, bringing the arms to the overhead position; return to the Starting Position with the arms falling naturally toward the back and pulling up in convex curves (Cts 5-2-3).

Repeat, with the twist opening to the left and the weight falling on the L leg.

Note: In resolving the transition between the twist descent and the beginning of the forward swing, the body moves naturally downward and backward with the arms as they fall.

Variation II: The above, with additional rebounds.

Count: Six measures of 3 beats each. Count in aggregate 3s.

Tempo: 112 (Slightly faster than above).

Starting Position: Same as above.

Phrase: Swing forward and up (Cts 1-3), swing downward and back (Cts 2-2-3), swing forward and up (Cts 3-2-3); twist and drop on R foot with slight rebound (Cts 4-2-3); drop again on R foot with slight rebound (Cts 5-2-3); drop once more on R foot (Ct 6-) and rebound back into Starting Position, letting arms fall downward and backward (Cts -2-3).

Repeat with twist to left, dropping on L foot.

Note: The Swinging Series can also be counted in a slow 4/4 time, with similar emphasis on the rhythmic interplay of falling and recovering.

14. UP AND FORWARD, DOWN AND BACK

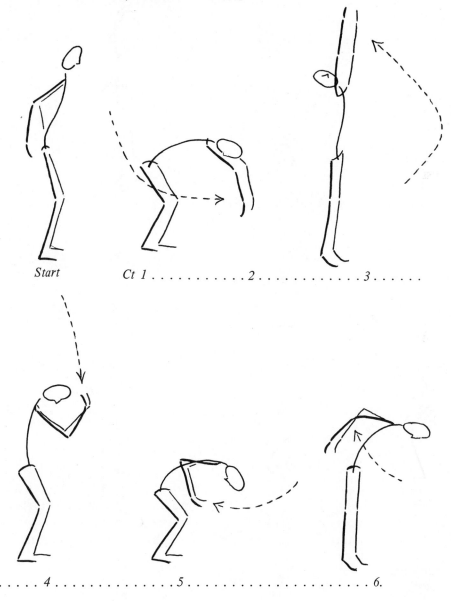

Start   Ct 1 . . . . 2 . . . . 3 . . . . . .

. . . . . 4 . . . . 5 . . . . 6.

Variation I: Twist and Rebound

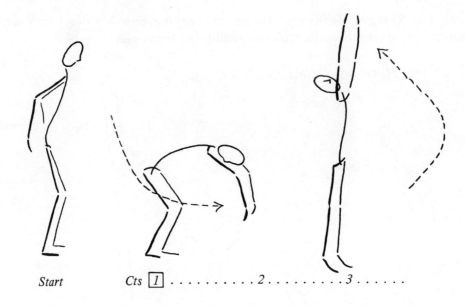

Start   *Cts* 1 . . . . 2 . . . . 3 . . . . . .

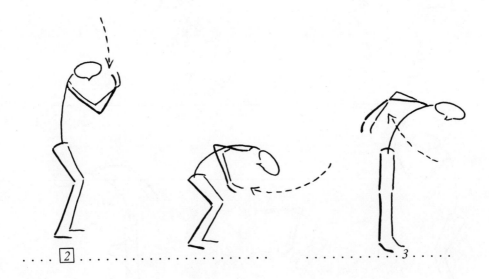

. . . . 2 . . . . 3 . . . . .

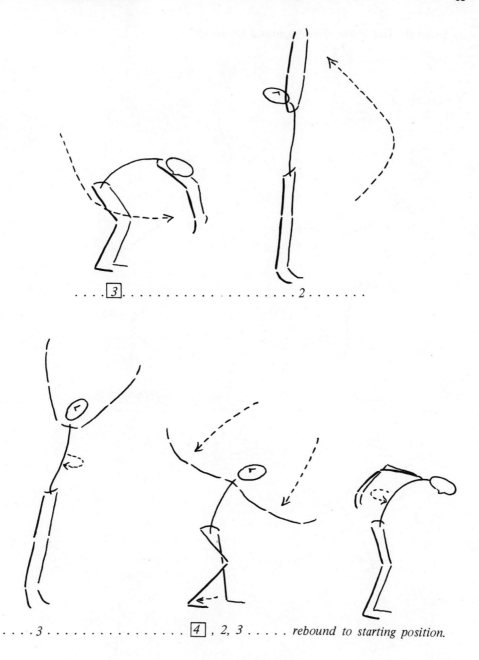

..... ③ .... 2 ......

..... 3 .... ④ , 2, 3 ..... *rebound to starting position.*

Variation II: The Above, with Additional Rebounds

Same as Variation I
for counts $\boxed{1}$ *, 2, 3,*
$\boxed{2}$ *, 2, 3,* $\boxed{3}$ *, 2, 3 . . . .*

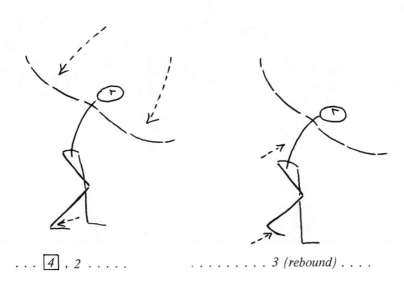

. . . $\boxed{4}$, 2 . . . . 3 *(rebound)* . . . .

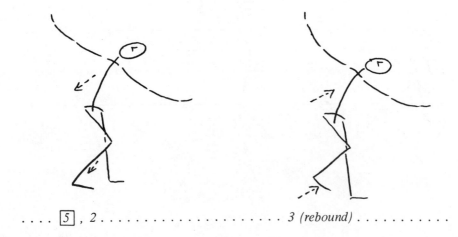

. . . . $\boxed{5}$, 2 . . . . 3 *(rebound)* . . . .

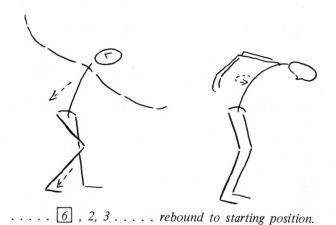

. . . . . $\boxed{6}$, 2, 3 . . . . . *rebound to starting position.*

15. VERTICAL TORSO AND HEAD SWINGS: Half-Circles

Count: One-swing phrase of 4 beats, in 4/4 time.

Tempo: 60 (Moderately slow) *Music Quality:* Sustained, flowing.

Starting Position: Facing front, legs apart and turned out at about 45-degree angle, arms relaxed at the sides.

Phrase: With exhalation of the breath, allow only the torso to fall (with the arms hanging naturally from the shoulders) in a curve to the right, then down across the body in an arc that pulls up over the L bent knee sideways. The knees bend and stretch according to the body's needs. It is necessary to pull up *sideways,* i.e., with the shoulders remaining in frontal position and the head dropping to the side over the shoulder, so that a body stretch is achieved simultaneously with the action. The breath is exhaled on the downward drop (Cts 1-2), inhaled on the upward sideways pull (Cts 3-4). Then repeat the movement, pulling up to the right, etc.

Note: This preliminary exercise may be done several times without music for the purpose of clarifying the role of the breath and the movement's natural rhythmic phrasing.

Variation I: Vertical Half-Circles with Single Arms.

Count, Tempo, and *Music Quality:* Same as above.

Repeat the movement described above adding arms: Falling to the right, the R arm now follows the body motion, crossing in front and pulling up sideways to the left over the shoulder and head. The stretch is thereby increased, as well as the sense of the body's weight. Reverse direction, using the other arm.

Note: Both feet remain on the floor when first executing the exercise, but with the increase of body pull to one side, the opposite leg is lifted off the floor.

Variation II: Whole Vertical Circles. From these half-circles with single arms, the movement is easily expanded into whole vertical circles with both arms. At the highest point, movement is dramatically suspended overhead, face turned up, arms lifted parallel. The full vertical circle comprises falling sideways to the right with acceleration and knee bend, crossing low in front of the body, pulling up sideways to the left with knee bend, and continuing upward with deceleration to a high suspension, from which one may circle again to the right, or reverse direction.

15. VERTICAL TORSO AND HEAD SWINGS: Half-Circles

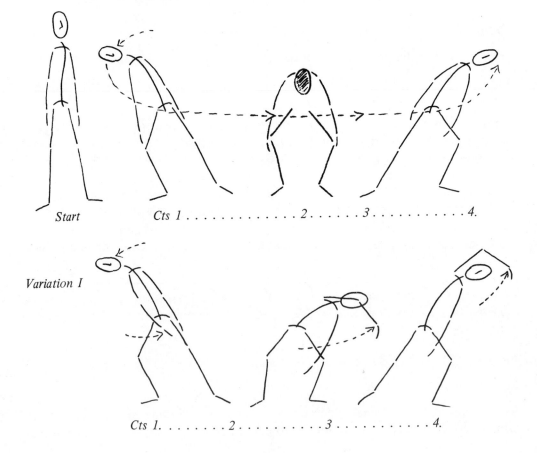

Start   *Cts 1* . . . . *2* . . . . . . *3* . . . . *4.*

Variation I

Cts 1. . . . . *2* . . . . *3* . . . . *4.*

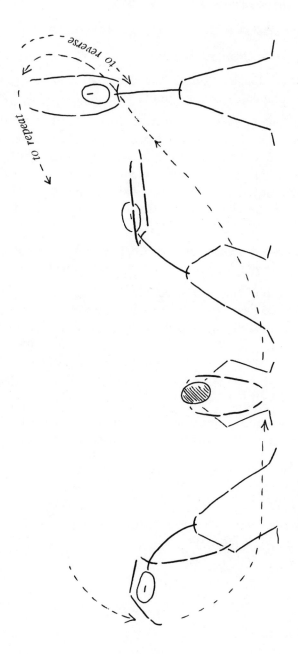

Variation II: Whole Vertical Circles

16. CENTER SWINGS WITH SIDEWAYS DROPS

Count: Three phrases of 6 beats each, in 3/4 time.

Tempo: 96   *Music Quality:* Vigorous, full-toned.

Starting Position: Facing front, legs well apart and turned out at about 45-degree angle. Arms extended to sides at shoulder height, fingers extended without tension.

Phrase 1: Downward swing of arms, ending crossed in front of chest (Cts 1-3). Knees bend out and down on impulse of Ct 1, and gradually stretch to straightness on Cts 2-3. Swing arms back to sideways open position (Cts 4-6). Knees bend on impulse of Ct 4 and subsequently straighten on Cts 5-6. Breath is exhaled on downward motions and inhaled on upward "recovery" motions. Emphasis is given to the changing momentum of the fall and recovery (acceleration-deceleration).

Repeat these center swings several times before preceeding with the sideways drops to establish (and feel) the natural dynamics of the movement.

Phrase 2: Swing once more into center (Cts 1-3). On the next open movement, the body drops sideways to the right with the arms opening and the R knee bending, foot and knee well turned out for support (Cts 4-6). The movement flows in succession through the torso, arms, neck, head. The whole body is now tilted sideways, and the weight is mainly on the R leg. Breath, as before, is exhaled on downward drop of arms sideways, after which there is a sense of suspension when the body comes to the outward terminal point of the swing.

Phrase 3: Swing once more into center, weight shifting back, arms returning to cross position (Cts 1-3), and repeat the sideways drop, falling now to the left (Cts 4-6).

Repeat the entire exercise several times.

Variation: Swing. The above with intensified sideways drops which lift the opposite leg off the floor. The suspension is now greater, the sense of the body being sustained midair is more intense.

16. CENTER SWINGS WITH SIDEWAYS DROPS

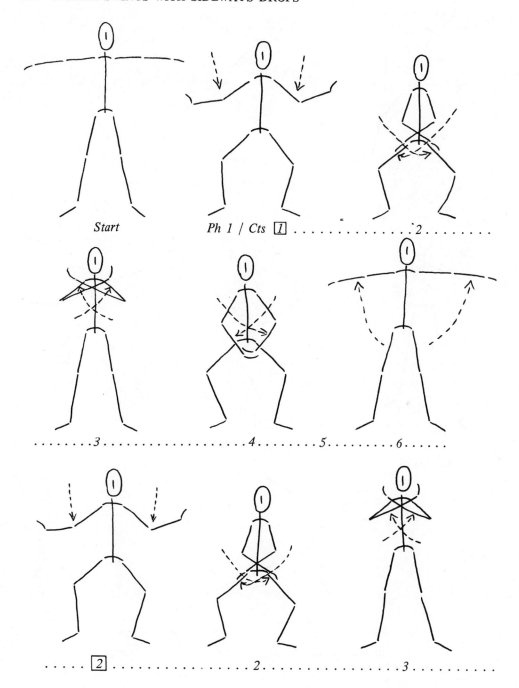

Start   *Ph 1 / Cts* ⬚1 . . . . 2 . . . .

. . . . 3 . . . . 4 . . . . 5 . . . . 6 . . . . . .

. . . . . ⬚2 . . . . 2 . . . . 3 . . . .

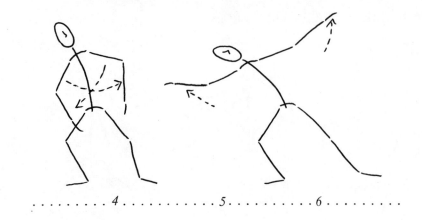

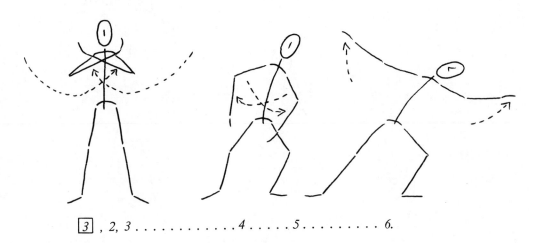

Variation: Swing

Intensified fall to side, opposite leg lifts (Ct 6)

17. SWINGS WITH VERTICAL CIRCLE PATTERNS

A center swing with a sideways drop followed by circular patterns involving directional changes.

Count: Five phrases of 6 beats each. Counting should be: 1-2-3-4-5-6, 2-2-3-4-5-6, 3-2-3-4-5-6, etc., to differentiate the phrases.

Tempo: 96 *Music Quality:* Resonant.

Starting Position: Facing front, legs well apart and turned out at about 45-degree angle. Arms crossed in front of body.

Phrase 1: Swing out (Cts 1-3); swing in (Cts 4-6).

Phrase 2: With next outward swing drop body to right (Cts 2-2-3) with increasing intensity of falling so that the L arm swings upward into an overhead arc, pulled by the momentum of the fall (Cts 4-5). On Ct 6, the sideways pull is changing to a falling motion, in which the torso rolls over from a flat sideways position to a down-swing.

Phrase 3: With both arms above the head, the body continues to drop with increasing speed and, circling down (Cts 3-2-3), continues the swing, and begins to mount toward the left, slowing into vertical suspension (Cts 4-5-6).

Phrase 4: At the height of the upward curve, the body begins to fall to the right again with increasing speed, from which it rises with decreasing speed to the left to a halfway point of the circle. R foot pulls slightly off the floor.

Phrase 5: At this point, the direction is reversed: the body drops toward the floor again, and rising with decreasing speed toward the right, comes to a point of suspension as the phrase ends, in balance, arms overhead, feet equally bearing weight. From this overhead position, the arms are ready to fall downward across the chest for a repeat of the center swing and subsequent movements.

Repeat the entire exercise several times with *alternate* sideways drops, once each direction has been mastered.

17. SWINGS WITH VERTICAL CIRCLE PATTERNS

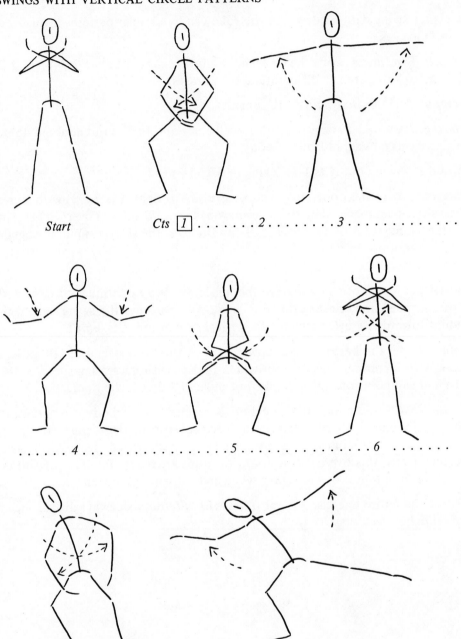

Start   *Cts* ☐1 . . . . 2 . . . . 3 . . . .

. . . . . . 4 . . . . 5 . . . . 6 . . . .

. . . . ☐2 . . . . 2 . . . . 3 . . . .

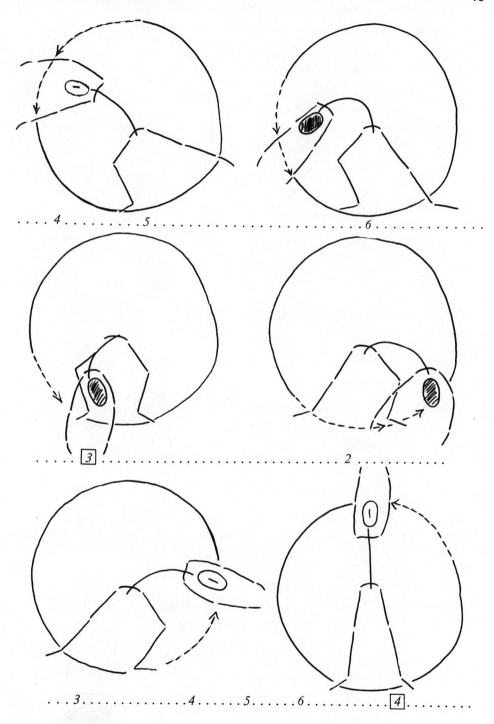

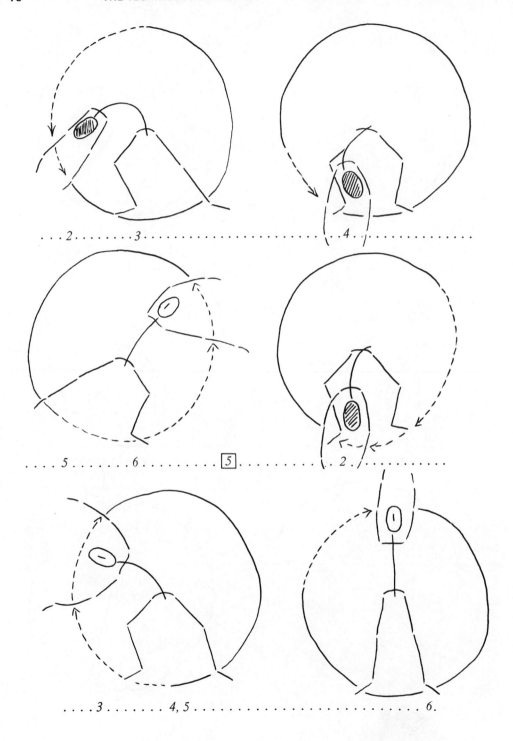

. . . . 2 . . . . 3 . . . . 4 . . . .

. . . . 5 . . . . 6 . . . . 5 . . . . 2 . . . .

. . . . 3 . . . . 4, 5 . . . . 6.

18. CENTER SWING WITH OVERDROP AND REBOUND

Count: Two phrases of 4 beats each.

Direction: Vertical and sideways.

Tempo: 52 (Moderately slow)   *Music Quality:* Strong, sustained.

Starting Position: Feet apart. Legs turned out at a 45-degree angle. Body facing front, arms open at shoulder height, palms facing front with thumbs relaxed. Knees straight without tension.

Phrase 1: With a downward and inward swing of the arms, the knees bend outward over the toes (Ct 1) and then straighten as the arms, crossing, rise in curves over the head (Ct 2). Breath is inhaled on the upward stroke, and is now about to be exhaled with the "overdrop." The overdrop consists of a falling motion to the right in which the torso bends sharply to the side as the arms open and fall (Ct 3). Knees bend outward over the toes, with emphasis on right side. Rebound (Ct 4), in which the arms pull up sideways once more and the body returns to the Starting Position. Breath is inhaled with movement.

Phrase 2: The same swing under, lift, drop, and rebound with the fall to the left side.

Exercise 18 The Overdrop (Count 3) seen from above: Penelope Hill

18. CENTER SWING WITH OVERDROP AND REBOUND

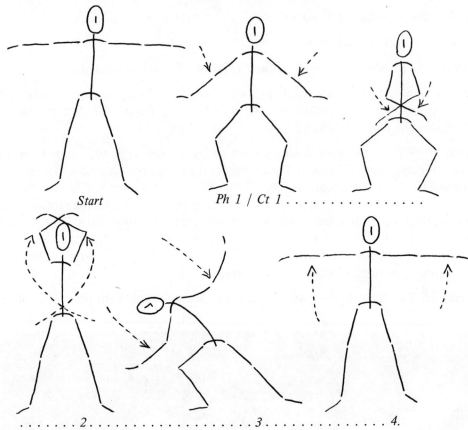

Start   *Ph 1 / Ct 1 . . . .*

. . . . 2 . . . . 3 . . . . 4.

Ph 2 / Repeat sequence on left side.

19. SINGLE ARM AND SIDE OVERDROP AND REBOUND

Count: Two phrases of 6 beats each (right and left).

Direction: Circular-Vertical.

Tempo and *Music Quality:* Same as above.

Starting Position: Feet apart. Legs turned out at a 45-degree angle. Body facing front, arms open at shoulder height, palms facing front with thumbs relaxed. Knees straight without tension.

Phrase 1: R arm turns over, twisting forward and down, from the shoulder with simultaneous bend of knees, impulse coming from R leg. Body curves forward-downward with the movement, twisting inward as the swing dips, and R knee turns in slightly with drop, heel being pulled off the floor (Ct 1). As the swing takes hold with a shift of weight to the left side, the body rises (successionally) with the curve of the arm, which has swept fully across center and is now lifting circularly toward the left (Ct 2). The swing now reaches its greatest height, with a stretching up of the body to the top of the curve, arm high overhead (Ct 3), in a brief suspension. On Ct 4, body and arm drop to the right and R knee returns to an open bent position (over the toes), the leg catching the falling body's weight. Weight is now principally over R leg and L leg is fully stretched (no knee bend) with heel slightly off the floor. Rebound on Ct 5, bringing R arm up into open position which is maintained in a suspension for Ct 6, as in Starting Position. Care should be taken to keep the hips in the same plane as the shoulders. Breath is inhaled on upward sweep of the swing and exhaled on drop, then inhaled with rebound and exhaled as other arm recommences the movement down. Successional movement of the arm on lift as well as on drop.

Phrase 2: The same swing down, up, overhead, drop, rebound with L arm and body involvement.

Suggested Repetition: Alternate successively for practice.

Variation I: Parallel Action of Leg and Arm. The leg now joins the working arm in parallel motion, the other arm remaining extended to the side. As the R arm swings up into the curve of the lift on Ct 2, the R leg does likewise and is suspended in the air on Ct 3 in a circular extension. It then drops with the body and arm back to its own side in the open falling position on Ct 4, with a relaxed sideways drop. The pelvis is lifted forward and up in the design of the curve, both knees are bent and open sideways, and the R knee is turned out sufficiently to stabilize the body's weight. Rebound to open center position, with legs resuming initial stance on Cts 5-6.

Repeat on the left.

Variation II: Using Both Arms, Fall to Opposite Side. Bring both arms down crossing them (Ct 1), then raise both arms in the circular pattern simultaneously with the lift of the R leg (Ct 2). Come to the peak suspension overhead as the leg is opening in the circular pattern to the right (Ct 3). As the R leg drops to the floor, the torso falls to the left, away from the R leg, arms dropping naturally to the sides, as both knees bend (Ct 4). Rebound to center with arms almost resuming their side position (Cts 5-6). Repeat by gathering up the L leg, both arms crossing and lifting to the peak suspension, then drop the L leg to its side while body falls to the right.

Suggested Repetition: Alternate patterns.

19. SINGLE ARM AND SIDE OVERDROP AND REBOUND

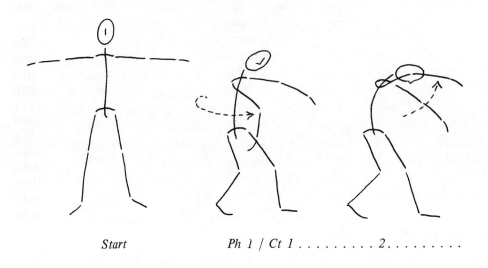

Start   *Ph 1 / Ct 1* . . . . *2* . . . .

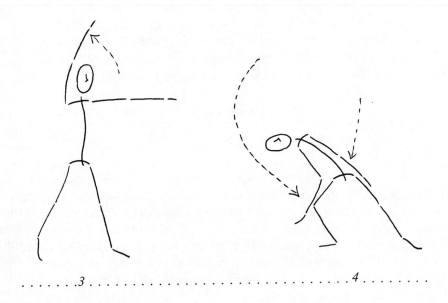

. . . .*3* . . . .*4* . . . .

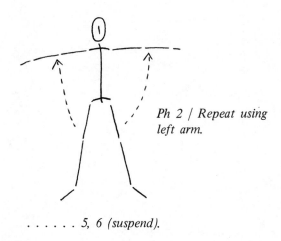

Ph 2 / Repeat using left arm.

. . . . . . *5, 6 (suspend).*

Variation I

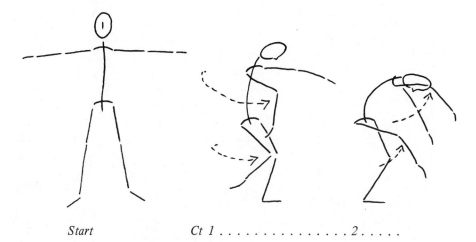

Start   *Ct 1 . . . . 2 . . . . .*

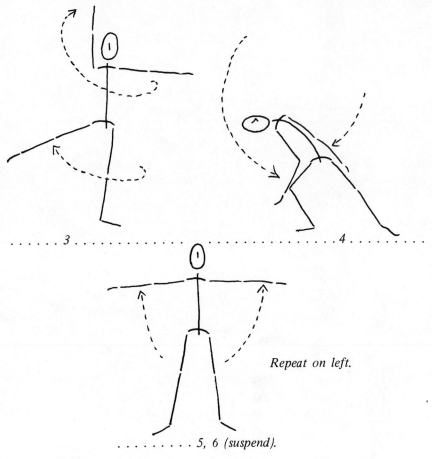

. . . . 3 . . . . 4 . . . .

Repeat on left.

. . . . 5, 6 *(suspend).*

Variation II

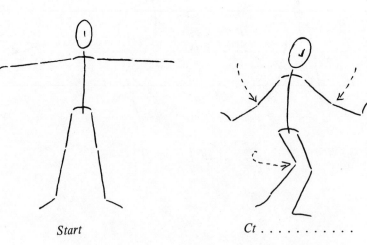

Start   *Ct* . . . .

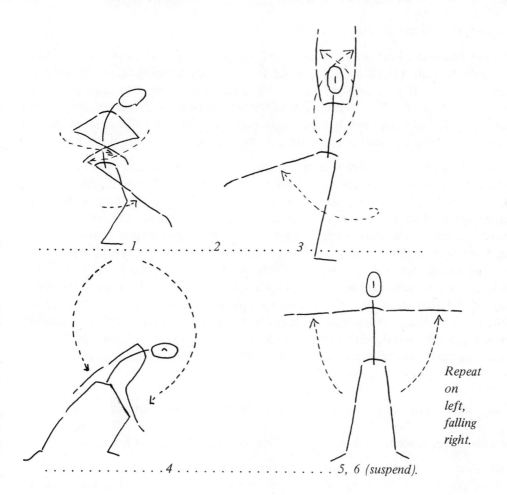

Repeat
on
left,
falling
right.

........1............2..........3 ....

..............4..................5, 6 (suspend).

20. FIGURE EIGHTS: Alternate Sides

A Figure Eight is essentially a double looping swing of the arm (arms) in conjunction with the entire body. The same dynamics prevail as for all body swings. When performed with one arm at a time, the "eight" lies on its side. When performed with both arms, the first loop of the "eight" is forward with a torso overbend and arms crossing then lifting; the second loop, a backward arching of the body with arms opening and falling, then lifting.

Count: A phrase of 8 beats.

Direction: Sideways.

Tempo: 86 *Music Quality:* Sustained.

Starting Position: Feet widely apart. Legs turned out at a 45-degree angle. Body facing front with weight on R leg, knee flexed, body bending from the waist toward the right, R arm outstretched at shoulder height, head in same direction, face tilted upward. The L arm is held without tension in a convex curve at its own side. The hips are slightly forward in the same plane as the shoulders and the movement pattern, although alternating to the far sides, is executed frontally.

Phrase: Lifting head, body, R arm and hand (with palm up and open) in a deep, wide curve to the far right (Ct 1), come to the crest of a sideways figure eight (Ct 2), then drop arm, head, body in an over-curve, crossing through center with gathering momentum (Ct 3); looping upward to the left now, lift the R arm far across the body in a second curve (Ct 4). With the body's weight now over the L leg, knee flexed, the R arm mounts with gradually decreasing energy toward the peak of the second loop (Cts 5-6). This action stretches the R leg so that the toes are barely touching the floor. Now a falling motion will occur in the direction of the first loop, i.e., the R arm sweeps down across the body toward the right (Ct 7). Again, momentum gathers as the body is opening sideways, weight on R leg, knee flexed, with the arm pulling in the under-curve and mounting to the far right (Ct 8). With the fulfillment of this movement, the figure eight is now ready to be repeated without pause.

Note: Breath is inhaled and exhaled naturally on up-down motions.

Suggested Repetition: A minimum of 4 on each side (right and left).

Variation: The same arm and body movement with the leg opposite to outwardly pulling arm lifted off the floor in a moderately high extension when the intensity of the momentum is increased.

20. FIGURE EIGHTS: Alternate Sides

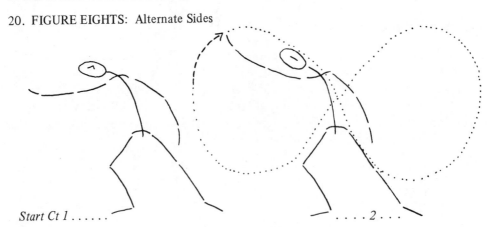

Start Ct 1 . . . . 2 . . .

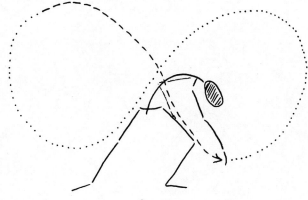

. . . . *3* . . . .

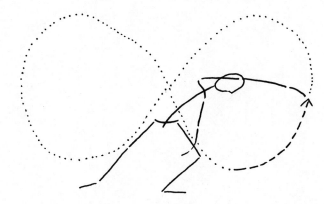

. . . . *4* . . . . *5* . . . .

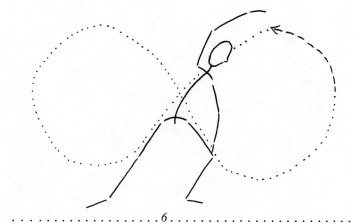

. . . . *6* . . . .

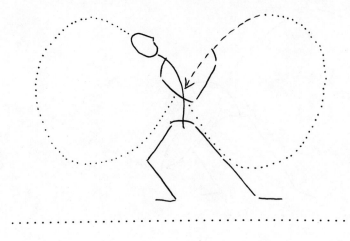

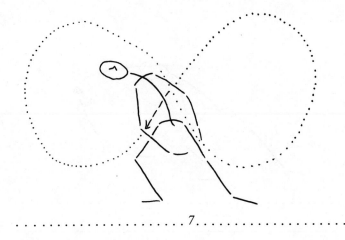

7.

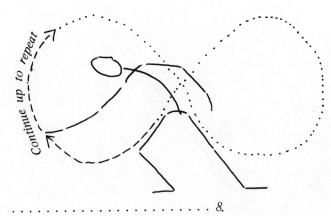

8.

Variation: Opposite Leg Lifted in Extension when Momentum Increases.

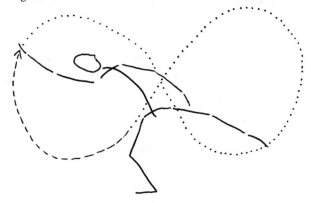

21. FIGURE EIGHTS: Both Arms

Count: A phrase of 6 beats, with 3-count preparation.

Direction: Forward-over, up, dropping back, up.

Tempo: 86 *Music Quality:* Sustained.

Starting Position: Feet apart. Legs turned out at a 45-degree angle. Body facing front with weight evenly divided. Arms at sides, palms facing out.

Preparation: With impulse in knees, lift both arms sideways; inhale breath and allow the movement to flow through neck and head as well as shoulders (Cts 1-2). Arms are now extended upward and outward, about to reach the crest of the arc on Ct 3, palms about to turn over.

Phrase: Swing arms down and across, dropping torso and head forward and in, bending knees over the feet while arms cross in front of the body (Ct 1). The arms are now lifting and bringing the body up with them (Ct 2). Breath, which was exhaled on center drop is now being inhaled. On Ct 3, the center pull reaches its crest with arms overhead in gradually separating curves. The body is pulled high again, and is in suspension, ready to fall. This time, the fall (Ct 4) is backward and open, with the hips pulled forward and knees out to balance the body properly; the arms have dropped successively to their sides, the head is thrown back. The swing now reverses itself with the arms and body rebounding back, palms up, to the Preparatory Position (Cts 5 and 6).

Note: The Center Figure Eights (Both Arms) are broad sweeping motions with full torso bends forward and backward. Arms always move successively on lifts and drops, with hands turning easily in-down and over-up.

21. FIGURE EIGHTS: Both Arms

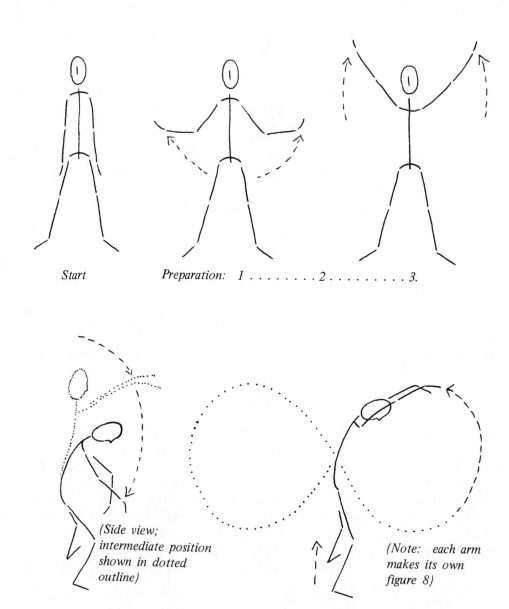

Start   Preparation: 1 . . . . 2 . . . . 3.

(Side view; intermediate position shown in dotted outline)

(Note: each arm makes its own figure 8)

Ct 1 . . . . 2, 3 . . . .

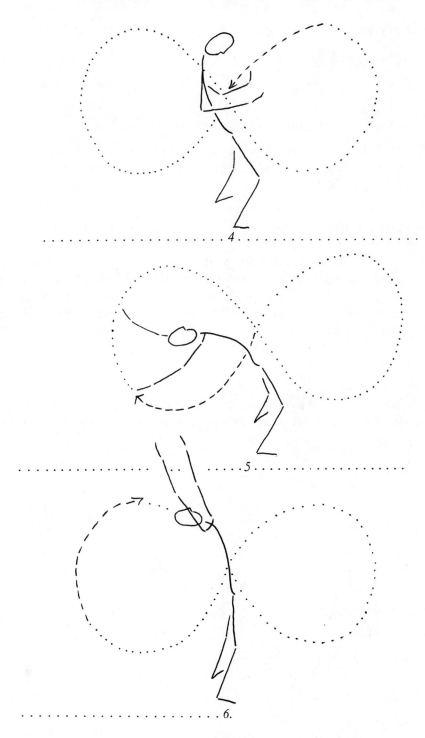

22. HORIZONTAL TORSO SWINGS: Half-Circles[1]

Count: Two phrases of 6 beats each.

Direction: A successional fall, through the torso only, in a backward horizontal curve from side to side.

Tempo: 48 (Slow)   *Music Quality:* Sustained and resonant.

Starting Position: Feet apart in wide stance. Legs turned out at 45-degree angle. Body facing front with weight evenly placed on both legs. Arms extended to the sides at shoulder height with slight backward curve of elbows and wrists.

Phrase 1: With exhalation of breath, bend R knee, drop torso and head to right side and with an accelerating falling motion swing toward the back (Cts 1-2), arriving at center back with face looking up, torso far back, and both knees well bent, hips lifted, heels on floor (Ct 3); continue the falling-swinging motion toward the left side, pulling up with the torso sideways and inhaling breath (Cts 4-6). The weight is now on the L leg with the head falling naturally to the side, the arms remain extended in long curves, while the R leg, though not straightened completely, stretches from the ankle.

Phrase 2: Reverse direction.

Note: The hips are pulled forward and up, with the thighs absorbing the support of the body's weight. In this way, no strain is put on the lumbar region of the back. The Half-Circle Torso Swings are used as a preparation for the Full Circle Torso Swings.

22. HORIZONTAL TORSO SWINGS: Half-Circles

Start   Ct 1 . . . .

[1]Similar to the first movements of Doris Humphrey's *Circular Descent.*

(Seen from
the side)

. . . . .2 . . . . .3 . . . .

Pull up with torso;
inhale.

. . . . .4,5 . . . . 6.

23. HORIZONTAL TORSO SWINGS: Full Circles

Count: Two phrases of 6 beats each.

Direction: Movement remains approximately shoulder height throughout. The
circle is described by one arm at a time. Starting from the side position, the arm
swings forward, then to the other side, then to the back across the body, return-

ing to its original position. Counter-clockwise with the R arm, clockwise with the L arm.

Tempo: 48 (Slow)   *Music Quality:* Sustained and resonant.

Starting Position: Feet apart in wide stance. Legs turned out at a 45-degree angle. Body facing front with arms at sides in natural convex curves. Weight evenly divided.

Preparation: On "and" preceding Ct 1, lift and stretch R arm sideways to shoulder height, L arm remaining at side, fingers resting lightly on L thigh; R arm is at shoulder height with torso and head pulled sideways with it. Weight has shifted to R leg with bend of knee; L leg stretches almost straight.

Phrase 1: With strong impulse, begin forward circle with body and arm coordinating, R arm moving counter-clockwise toward the front (Ct 1). Knees bend out over feet, and weight remains equally divided (Ct 2). By Ct 3, the R arm is passing over to the left side and leg weight shifts left. Continuing the circle, the torso begins to lean backward, and there is a simultaneous forward shift of the hips, stabilizing the weight equally over both legs. The R arm is curving over the head on the backward lean (Ct 4). Now the backward pull of the arm is in full effect and the torso is on its way to complete the circular motion. By Ct 6, the weight is again pulled to the right with R arm completing the circle.

Repeat with the right arm 3 or 4 times.

Phrase 2: Continuing in alternate direction, on Ct 6-"and", drop the R arm with an immediate pull of the L arm to the left. Weight shifts to the left side, and the movement repeats in a clockwise direction with the L arm describing the circle.

Variation: Three-Quarter Circle Ending with a Vertical Arm Thrust. Follow the above directions with a slightly increased speed of the swing so that, by Ct 3, the torso and the R arm are already back of the hips. On Ct 4, bend the R elbow sharply sideways at shoulder height, hand facing front, and deepen knee bend. On Ct 5, the R arm is slowly pushing upward supported solidly by the torso and the knees and torso are gradually straightening. The head is now looking upward past the hand. The vertical thrust is completed by Ct 6.

Repeat to other side: On Ct 6-"and", let the R arm drop toward the R thigh, lift L arm to its side, shifting weight to left, and repeat with a clockwise motion preceding the vertical thrust with the L arm. When the movement has been repeated enough to assure smoothness and control, both arms are used in the final upward thrust (Cts 5-6), bringing the body to its full standing height to prepare for the Center Drop, Rebound, and Circular Successions (Exercise 24).

Exercise 23 Full Circle Variation, Vertical Thrust (Count 5): Gail Corbin

23.   HORIZONTAL TORSO SWINGS: Full Circles

Start   *Ct And* . . . .

. . . . . *1, 2* . . . . *3* . . . .

. . . . *4, 5* . . . . *6.*

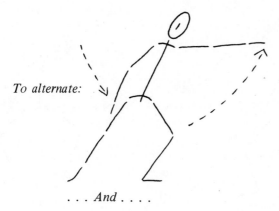

To alternate:

. . . And . . . .

Variation: Three-Quarter Circle Ending with a Vertical Arm Thrust

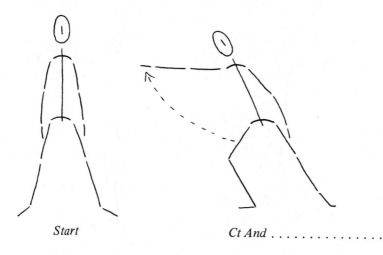

Start

Ct And . . . .

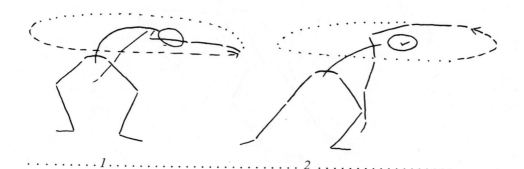

. . . . 1 . . . . 2 . . . .

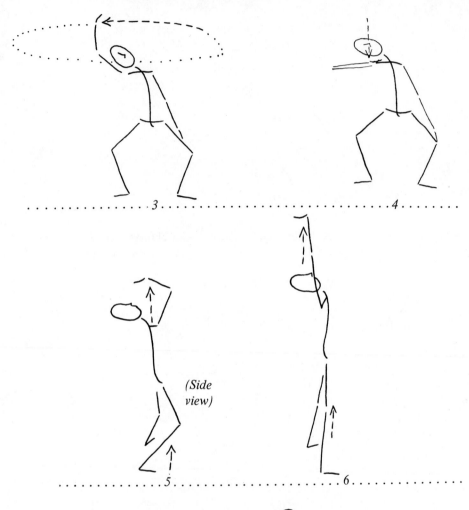

. . . . 3 . . . . 4 . . . .

(Side
view)

. . . . 5 . . . . 6 . . . .

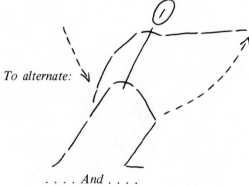

To alternate:

. . . . And . . . .

24. CENTER DROP, REBOUND, AND CIRCULAR SUCCESSIONS

Continuation of Exercise 23. The Circular Succession is one of the most lucid examples of the Humphrey Fall/Recovery theory combined with Successional Movement. Circular Successions constitute the basic movement language of *Water Study*, symbolizing in their rise and fall the tidal motion of the sea. They demand considerable strength in the thighs, a forward positioning of the pelvis throughout most of the action, and steady balance.

Count, Tempo, and *Music Quality:* Same as above.

Direction: Forward-down-up; forward-down-back-up.

Starting Position: Feet well apart, arms overhead, body lifted. Focus forward and up.

Center Drop and Rebound

With exhalation of breath, let the torso fall directly down with arms facing the body and bending successionally (elbows, wrists, fingers) until torso is rounded over, knees bent over the feet, fingers touching the floor, and head dropped completely (Cts 1-3). Rebound, reversing direction of arms, hands, body, and head with decreasing speed (Cts 4-6). By Ct 6, the body and arms have regained their previous height and are ready to begin the circular succession.

Circular Succession

Starting at the height of the arm and body stretch, the arms start falling forward (ferris-wheel fashion) with palms facing in, the knees bend forward and the body curves over (Cts 1-2). Breath is gradually exhaled. As the arms begin to pass alongside the legs, the hips begin to tilt forward, the shoulders pull back, and the action goes into reverse. The head is still curved forward. With inhalation of breath, the weight is absorbed by the legs, thighs, and hips (Ct 3); as the torso begins to open, the head falls back with the arms, which sweep backward, palms open, and the upward pull begins (Ct 4). With decreased speed the body is now lifting, the weight being propelled forward into the thighs and pelvis, with the arms pulling upward alongside the torso as the body stretches to its full height (Cts 5-6). At the peak, the feet press into the floor, the hips are placed beneath the shoulders, and the body steadies itself in perfect equilibrium.

Repeat, starting with center fall.

Exercise 24 Circular Succession (Count 4): Mira Pospisil

Variation: Single Arm Successions. Follow directions for Circular Succession, but use only one arm at a time, leaving the other arm extended upward in a more or less fixed vertical position while the moving arm describes the circle and the body follows accordingly.

Repeat, alternating arms.

Note: Exercises 24 and Variation may be combined in alternating groups of movement. (First drop, rebound, and produce succession with two arms, then drop, rebound, and produce succession with single arms.) Both exercises are concluded with the upward motion.

24. CENTER DROP, REBOUND, AND CIRCULAR SUCCESSIONS

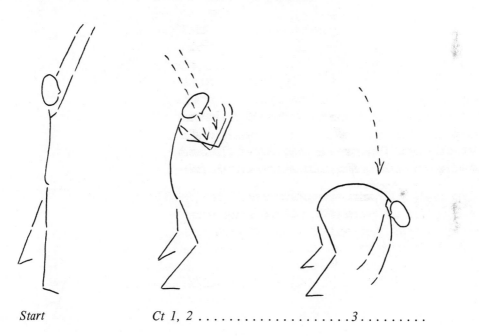

Start   Ct 1, 2 . . . . .3 . . . .

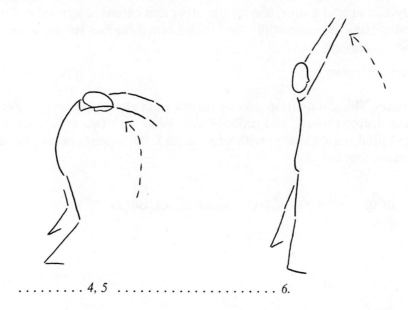

. . . . 4, 5 . . . . 6.

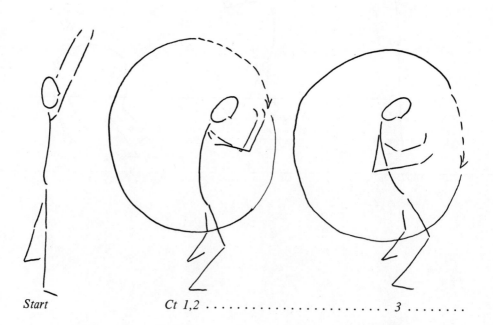

Start   *Ct 1,2* . . . . 3 . . . .

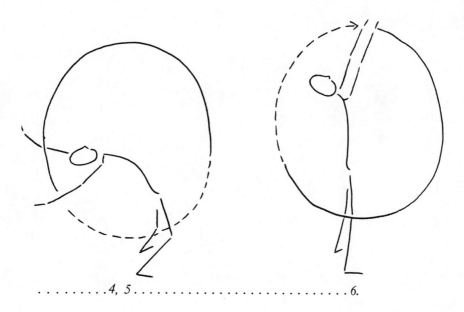

. . . . .4, 5. . . . . 6.

Variation: Single Arm Successions.

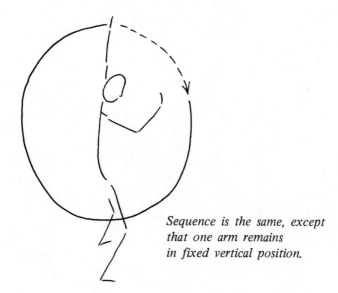

*Sequence is the same, except
that one arm remains
in fixed vertical position.*

Chapter 4

FLOOR WORK

INTRODUCTION

When Doris Humphrey wrote, "The modern dancer must . . . come down to the ground to establish his relationship with gravity and reality,"[1] she was referring to the new esthetic behind all modern dance, an esthetic which was following in the footsteps of the other modern arts. A rebellion had already started in music, architecture, painting, sculpture, and literature against the pseudo-romantic decadence of art in the late nineteenth century. This rebellion had been sparked, in part, by archeological discoveries of primitive art. Artists like Paul Klee, Constantin Brancusi, Georges Rouault, Henry Moore, Pablo Picasso, Jean Arp, Henri Matisse, and others were inspired by the primitive's use of bold colors, planal forms and non-representative spatial relationships. There was a vigor and healthy directness in the new art which broke radically with Impressionism and the effete, naturalistically representative painting and sculpture then in vogue. In architecture, music, and literature there were radical innovations as well.[2]

---

[1] Humphrey, "My Approach to the Modern Dance," p. 188.
[2] See Louis Horst's *Modern Dance Forms in Relation to the Other Modern Arts* (San Francisco: Impulse Publications, 1961; Reprint: Brooklyn, N.Y., Dance Horizons).

The new reality seized the modern dance in America, and the search for an esthetic related to primitive concepts led to a reinvestigation of space. The floor (ground) became a dance area of comparable importance with other levels—midspace and the air. Exercises were devised to explore the body's capacity to move freely on the floor, with a view of incorporating such movements into the fabric of a dance composition.

Several of the following floor exercises were devised by Doris Humphrey for the purposes of demonstrating her theories of opposition in the three planes of motion, and for strengthening the thighs in preparation for falls. The majority of the exercises described use the Fall and Recovery principles, along with Successional Movement, in a variety of positions designed to develop muscular strength and flexibility in the back, stomach, and legs.

It should be remembered that the basic "sitting position," which is the balance point for starting and recovering, is accomplished only when the body's weight is properly supported by torso placement directly over the ischial tuberosities—the "sitting" bones in the buttocks. The spine should be straight in the upright position, unless otherwise indicated. Exercises 1-3 may be performed to the same music in continuously unfolding sequences.

STRETCHES

25. SUCCESSIONAL BREATH MOVEMENT

A combined inner-thigh and torso stretch.

Count: Four phrases of 4 beats each.

Tempo: 52-54 *Music Quality:* Quiet, but slightly accented.

Starting Position: Sitting upright on the floor, holding the ankles, draw the heels together so that the feet touch and the knees are bent outward from the body. The elbows should be brought forward as much as possible to align with the knees. Back is held as straight as possible.

Preparation: Slowly bounce forward, with straight spine, returning to the vertical position 8 times; then drop over and bounce with rounded back 8 times. Repeat both sequences. Return to upright position.

Phrases 1-4: Exhaling the breath slowly, let the torso fall forward, head included, into a curve (Cts 1-4); recover with slow intake of breath to Starting Position (Cts 1-4); exhaling again, let the torso curve backward while the shoulders stay above the hips (Cts 1-4); inhaling, recover once more to the Starting Position (Cts 1-4).

Repeat, with 2 counts for each motion.

Repeat, with 1 count for each motion.

Suggested Repetition: A total of 4 times for the complete exercise in each tempo. Continue without break into next exercise.

Note: The movements of the torso are performed successionally with the breath as the initiating factor.

25. SUCCESSIONAL BREATH MOVEMENT

Start   Preliminary Motion: 8 bounces . . . . . return . . . .

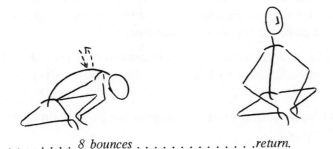

. . . . 8 bounces . . . . .return.

Ph 1 / Cts 1, 2, 3, 4 . . . . *1, 2, 3, 4* . . . . *Exhale 1, 2, 3, 4* . . . . . .

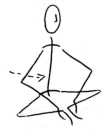

. . . Inhale 1, 2, 3, 4.

26. KNEE STRETCH: Forward and Up

An exercise for alignment of the spine and strengthening of the thighs.

Count: Three phrases of 8 beats each.

Tempo: 52-54   *Music Quality:* Quiet, but emphatic.

Starting Position: Sitting on the floor, knees together bent in front of the body, arms open sideways shoulder height, palms facing front, spine angled backward in an oblique straight line. Head is in alignment with spine. Toes touch the floor lightly. Keep shoulders in place throughout the movement.

Phrase 1: Extend the R leg upward until the knee is straight (Cts 1-2). Returning the R leg to Starting Position, change to L leg extension upward (Cts 3-4). Repeat once more.

Phrase 2: Repeat the kicking motion with the movement changing on every beat for a total of 8 Cts (8 kicks).

Phrase 3: Bring up bent leg and hold both legs extended straight in the air at the same angle for 8 beats.

Suggested Repetition: Once more in its entirety, then proceed without break into next exercise.

26. KNEE STRETCH

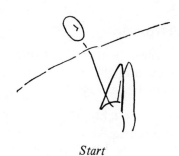

Start

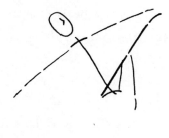

Ph 1 / Cts 1, 2 . . . . .

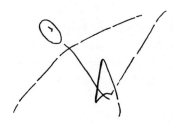

. . . . .3, 4.

Ph 2 / Repeat kicking for 8 counts.

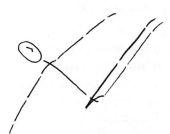

Ph 3 / Hold 8 counts.

27. OPPOSITIONAL THRUSTS

An exercise designed to develop awareness of natural oppositional motion of legs and arms.

Count: Two phrases of 8 beats each (both sides).

Tempo: 52-54   *Music Quality:* Accented with resonance.

Starting Position: Sitting on the floor with the knees bent in front of the body, feet on the floor. L arm is bent with elbow-to-hand straight alongside the L knee. R hand is on floor next to R hip. Body is curved over, head close to knees.

Phrase 1: On Ct 1, strike the L hand forward (arm straightens); at the same time the R leg thrusts forward on the floor (knee straightens). Arm and leg are parallel. Head follows the line of the lifted body which has been tilted slightly backward. Return to Starting Position (Ct 2). Repeat 4 times.

Phrase 2: Change arms and strike the R arm forward with L leg thrust, and return to position. Repeat 4 times.

Variation I: With strike of R leg and L arm, lift hips to horizontal position over the floor (Cts 1-2). The placement of the hips is high, inducing strain on the thigh muscles for support. R hand on the floor bears the weight of the upper body. Head is thrown back, face looking upward. Return to Starting Position (Cts 3-4). Repeat 4 times.

Repeat on other side.

Variation II: Parallel Thrusts.

Count: One phrase of 4 slow beats.

Starting Position: Same as above with the head dropped on the bent knees and both hands on the floor behind the hips.

Phrase: On Cts 1-2, thrust the knees forward, bringing the hips up, while stretching the body and head backward. The weight now rests on the hands and the balls of the feet with the heels raised. The line between the knees, hips, and head should be straight. On Cts 3-4, return to the closed position, dropping the hips and rounding the back.

Suggested Repetition: At least 4 times.

27. OPPOSITIONAL THRUSTS

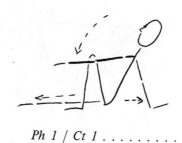

Start   *Ph 1 / Ct 1 . . . .*

. . . . 2.   *Repeat 4 x with left arm and right leg;*
then 4 x with right arm and left leg.

Variation I

Cts 1, 2 . . . . 3, 4.

Variation II: Parallel Thrusts

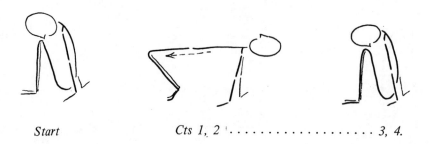

Start   *Cts 1, 2* .... *3, 4.*

28. LEG AND BODY STRETCHES WITH FALL/RECOVERY TIMING

Combining the demands of a total stretching with the dynamics of the fall, rebound, and suspension.

Count: Six phrases of 8 beats each, including rebound. Variations provide "rest" through change.

Tempo: 60   *Music Quality:* Accented, percussive.

Starting Position: On floor with legs and arms outstretched sideways. Weight over the "sitting bones." Torso is held erect as exercise starts.

Phrase 1: With arms extended sideways at shoulder height, bear forward with straight spine as low as possible without allowing buttocks to leave the floor, and bounce 8 times. Each bounce, as noted before, has the fall/recovery timing which implies variations in speed. On the 8th bounce, recover to vertical position, slowing up toward the zenith on 8-"and".

Phrase 2: Fall sideways to the right from the waist, L arm stretched in a curve framing the head, R arm dropping on R leg. Bounce 8 times, and rebound to upright center position on 8-"and".

Phrase 3: Fall toward left with R arm curving overhead and L arm on the L leg. Bounce 8 times with rebound on 8-"and", bringing both arms over head in parallel vertical lines.

Phrase 4: Bringing arms down in front and close to the body, bending elbows and keeping palms facing the torso, place elbows on the floor (Cts 1-4) and then stretch forward, pushing the elbows out as the hands press forward (palms out) close to the floor to make a breast-stroke motion forward and outward; at the same time flex the feet (Cts 5-8). The hands come to rest at the ankles or the toes, grasping either.

Phrase 5: Holding the feet, bounce 8 times forward and downward with rebound on 8-"and", returning to the Starting Position.

Phrase 6: Swing the L arm across toward R ankle, bending body and head over leg with extended back (Ct 1); rebound to Starting Position with arms outstretched (Ct 2). Swing R arm in same way toward L ankle (Ct 3); rebound to Starting Position (Ct 4). Swing L arm toward R ankle (Ct 5); rebound to center (Ct 6). Swing R arm toward L ankle (Ct 7); rebound to center (Ct 8).

Repeat the entire sequence.

28. LEG AND BODY STRETCHES WITH FALL/RECOVERY TIMING

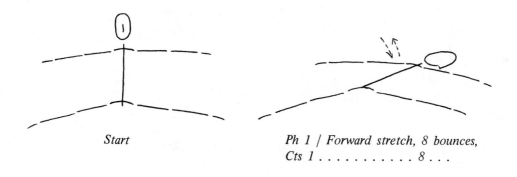

Start

Ph 1 | Forward stretch, 8 bounces,
Cts 1 . . . . 8 . . .

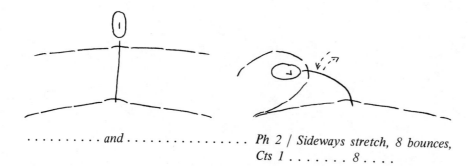

. . . . *and* . . . . *Ph 2 | Sideways stretch, 8 bounces,*
Cts 1 . . . . 8 . . . .

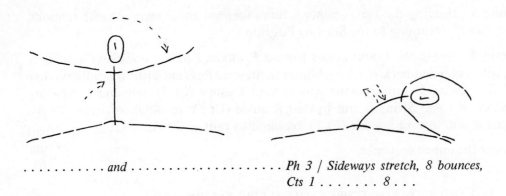

. . . . *and* . . . . *Ph 3 / Sideways stretch, 8 bounces,*
Cts 1 . . . . 8 . . .

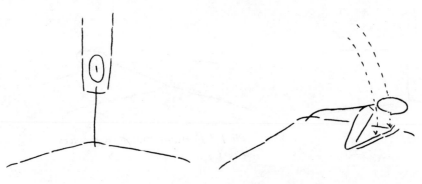

. . . . *and* . . . . *Ph 4 / Cts 1, 2, 3, 4* . . . .

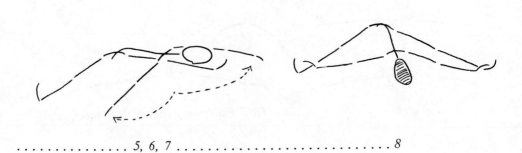

. . . . *5, 6, 7* *8*

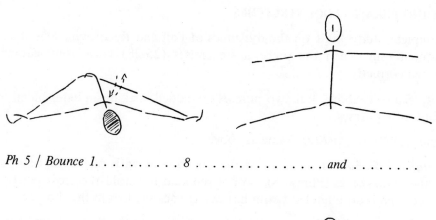

Ph 5 / Bounce 1. . . . . 8 . . . . and . . . .

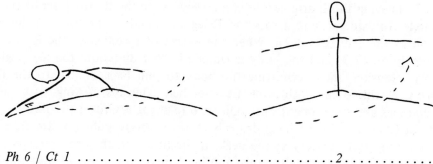

Ph 6 / Ct 1 . . . . 2 . . . .

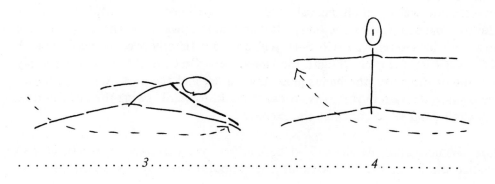

. . . . 3 . . . . 4 . . . .

. . . . Repeat, alternating arms to center on 8.

29. EIGHT-PHRASE FLOOR STRETCHES

A complete study built on the dynamics of Fall and Recovery. This should be attempted only when the preceding exercises (25-28) have been learned and executed correctly.

Count: Same as above, but two phrases are added, making an independent musical form of 8 phrases.

Tempo and *Music Quality:* Same as above.

Preparation: Follow directions for the Six Phrases with one exception: on Ct 7 of the cross-swings (Phrase 6), do not rebound but hold the cross position for Ct 8. R hand is on L ankle. L arm has swung backward from the shoulder.

Phrase 7: Leaving the L arm extended sideways, with the R arm describe the rim of a circle forward, passing across the R leg and bending the torso in the same direction as the arm (Cts 1-2). When the R arm is stretched to the R side (approximately on Ct 3) and the body is leaning in that direction, the legs begin to close with tension, thus permitting the body to pull back almost to the floor (Cts 4-5); at this point both arms are stretched sideways in long, soft curves, torso and legs are in a straight line. On Ct 6 (a slight retard in the music is suggested for Cts 6 and 7) the head drops back as the body pulls upward from the chest, reaching full recovery at the peak of the lift, with the arms stretched upward as well (Ct 7); the body, arms, and head now drop forward over the legs, which remain straight, hands touching the ankles (Ct 8).

Phrase 8: Pulling backward with a rounded body, draw the arms, elbows pulling, alongside the waist, simultaneously pulling up the knees (Cts 1-2); lift the arms sideways, palms up, with the body also stretching upward and the knees opening outward as in Exercise 25 (Cts 3-4). The arms are directly over the head in parallel lines (Ct 5), the back straight, the knees open. On Ct 6, the arms drop sharply in front of the body, the hands grasp the ankles, and the back remains straight. Three sharp staccato movements—forward, back, forward—swing the body in time with Cts 7-"and"-8 to conclude the exercise.

Note: While certain details should be clarified and corrected, it is advisable to practice the entire exercise without interruption to gain a sense of the study as a whole.

29. EIGHT-PHRASE FLOOR STRETCHES

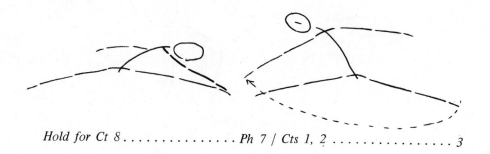

Hold for Ct 8 . . . . *Ph 7 / Cts 1, 2* *3*

. . . .*4*. . . . .*5*. . . . .

. . . .*6*. . . . .*7*. . . . .

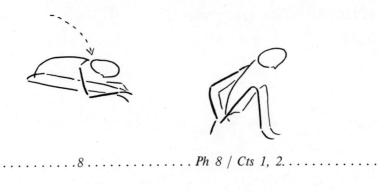

. . . . 8 . . . . *Ph 8 / Cts 1, 2.* . . . .

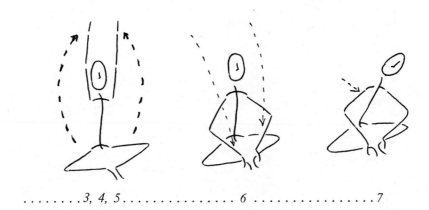

. . . . *3, 4, 5* . . . . *6* *7*

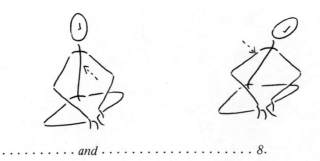

. . . . *and* . . . . *8.*

30. THIGH STRETCH

One of the most demanding exercises, the Thigh Stretch serves as a preparation for falls and half-falls in the center and at the barre.

Count: Three phrases of 6 beats each.

Tempo: 58 *Music Quality:* Resonant, strong.

Starting Position: Sitting on the feet, knees together, buttocks resting on the up-turned heels, body dropped over, rounded back, head down, hands resting on the floor beside knees.

Phrase 1: With intake of breath, slowly roll body backward successively until hips tilt up and forward and torso leans back at an extreme oblique angle. The arms have moved backward with the torso, the hands catching some of the body's weight on the floor to the rear of the feet (Cts 1-6).

Phrase 2: Bounce gently 3 times in this position, keeping the line of the body unbroken from knees to shoulders, and making sure that the hips remain lifted forward off the feet (Cts 1-3). Now take the hands off the floor and extend the arms forward at waist height in front of the body, palms facing in. Hold this position (Cts 4-6). The body's weight is now completely supported by the muscles in the thighs (quadriceps femoris).

Phrase 3: Release hips and return to the Starting Position, letting the breath out and releasing the torso successionally (Cts 1-6).

Suggested Repetition: 3 times in succession.

Variation: For further strengthening, perform the exercise in 4 phrases: bounce 6 times for Phrase 2, and hold the thigh stretch with arms off the floor for 6 beats for Phrase 3; Phrase 4 then becomes the release movement.

30. THIGH STRETCH

  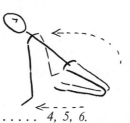

Start   *Ph 1 / Cts 1, 2, 3 . . . . 4, 5, 6.*

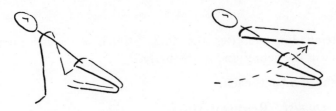

Ph 2 / Bounce gently: 1, 2, 3 . . . . Hold: 4, 5, 6.

Ph 3 / Release: 1–6.

ABDOMEN AND TORSO

The following five exercises (31-35) are designed to strengthen the abdominal and upper torso regions and thus ensure fluent body participation in all the Falling-Recovering and Successional Movements in the Humphrey Technique. A selection of at least two of these exercises should be included in every lesson.

31. BODY ROLL

A slow, horizontally-unfolding movement of the torso followed by an equally slow recovery.

Count: Two phrases of 8 beats each.

Tempo: 60   *Music Quality:* Flowing.

Starting Position: Sitting on the floor, legs together stretched forward, toes pointed, back rounded and dropped over the legs, hands at the sides of the legs, head close to knees. Breath expelled.

Phrase 1: Backward Descent. With intake of breath start unrolling the torso backward with head hanging down and arms sliding along the floor pulled back gently through the elbows and wrists (Cts 1-4). The body is now beginning the descent. The hands pass alongside the hips slightly in advance of the body pull. The fingers point in the direction of the backward fall, and the breath is being expelled slowly. As the hands catch the weight of the torso, the spine touches the floor, unfolding, with the head and shoulders last (Cts 5-8). Arms remain on the floor, extended upward and outward.

Phrase 2: Arched Ascent. With intake of breath, start lifting slowly by arching the torso and letting the head fall back. Shoulders should be relaxed and arms softly outstretched to maintain general balance; the legs, remaining straight, give the body leverage (Cts 1-4). It is important that the weight of the torso be carried through the chest as it lifts, and not relegated to the arms. The movement of the torso during the ascent is slow, with emphasis on the effort to resist gravitational pull; therefore the body is not moving at an even pace, and only reaches a nearly-upright position (just behind the hips) by Ct 4. The ascent continuing, the weight now approaches the highest point on Ct 5, and with the exhalation of the breath the body begins to fall with increasing speed over the legs (Cts 6-8).

Suggested Repetition: 3-4 times.

31. BODY ROLL

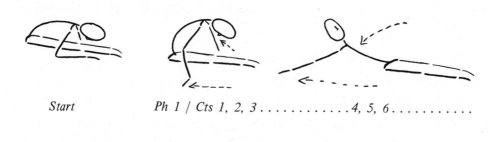

Start   Ph 1 / Cts 1, 2, 3 . . . . 4, 5, 6 . . . .

7 . . . . 8.   Ph 2 / Ct 1 . . . .

32. TORSO TWIST I

An accented descent of the torso, twisting successively through each shoulder.

Count: Four phrases of 8 beats each.

Tempo: 63   *Music Quality:* Rhythmically accented, fairly lively.

Starting Position: Sitting on the floor, back straight, legs together, knees firmly stretched, toes pointed, arms extended forward parallel to legs, palms facing in.

Phrase 1: Straight-Line Torso Descent. Keeping the back straight, begin to twist the torso to the right with the R shoulder tilted downward as the torso leans side-back (Ct 1); then twist to L side with L shoulder leaning farther back (Ct 2). Repeat this pattern with each shoulder pulling side-back on succeeding beats, making sure that the legs remain fully stretched to produce a counterweight to the body's pull (Cts 3-7). On Ct 7, the R shoulder should be close to the floor, head nearly touching, the entire torso suspended from the pelvis in as straight a line as possible; the arms are still forward, held without tension slightly above the hips. Hold this position for Ct 8.

Phrase 2: In this position, bounce softly backward on the R side, trying to touch the shoulder to the floor (Cts 1-7). There should be no change in the body align-ment from the beginning of this phrase to the end. Hold in suspension on Ct 8.

Phrase 3: Straight-Line Torso Ascent. Bring the R shoulder up and forward slight-ly (Ct 1), then the L shoulder (Ct 2), keeping the arms stretched forward in paral-lel lines as before. Repeat the motion with alternate shoulders until the body re-gains the sitting position by Ct 6; then start to fall forward with increasing speed over the legs on Cts 7 and 8, letting the knees relax outward.

Phrase 4: A Rest. With rounded back bounce in this relaxed position (Cts 1-4); then slowly and smoothly pull up to Starting Position (Cts 5-8).

Repeat the exercise with the L shoulder taking the initial movement on the de-scent and ascent.

Variation I: Use alternately flexed feet, flexing foot on the same side as the twist, for both the descent and ascent.

Variation II: The same movement set to a 6-Count Phrase with a hold on Ct 5 in the descent, a 3-Count relaxed forward drop on Phrase 4, and a 3-Count recovery to the Starting Position.

32. TORSO TWIST I

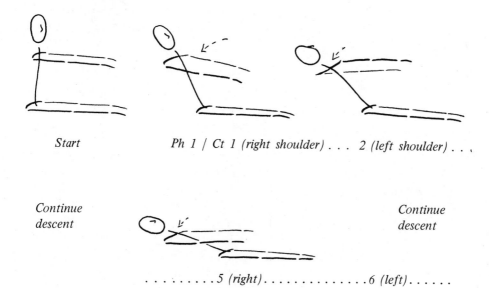

| Start | Ph 1 / Ct 1 (right shoulder) . . . 2 (left shoulder) . . . |

| Continue descent | | Continue descent |

. . . . 5 (right) . . . . 6 (left) . . . . . .

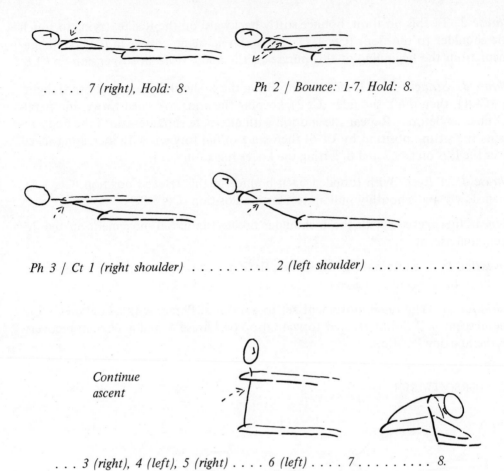

. . . . . *7 (right), Hold: 8.*   *Ph 2 / Bounce: 1-7, Hold: 8.*

Ph 3 / Ct 1 (right shoulder) . . . . *2 (left shoulder)* . . . .

*Continue
ascent*

. . . *3 (right), 4 (left), 5 (right)* . . . . *6 (left)* . . . . *7* . . . . *8.*

Ph 4 / Bounce: 1-4 . . . . *Recover: 5-8.*

Variation I

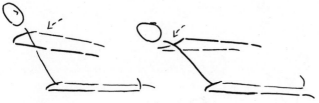

Descent: flex foot on side of twist

Ascent: flex foot on side of twist

Variation II: Same exercise in 6 count phrase.

33. TORSO TWIST II

A sharply accented thrusting of the knees toward and away from the chest.

Count: One phrase of 8 beats.

Tempo: 92   *Music Quality:* Strongly accented.

Starting Position: Sitting on the floor, knees bent, feet on floor. Body facing front, back slightly rounded. Elbows bent sideways at shoulder height and palms facing front. Focus forward.

Phrase: Pull knees up toward chest, lifting heels off floor; body contracts with pull and weight is on upper part of buttocks (Cts 1-2). Thrust arms forward and straighten legs, keeping them together, while twisting to the right on the R hip at an angle of approximately 45 degrees (Cts 3-4). Hands remain in the pushing position, palms facing front, wrists angled outward, fingertips almost touching. Now only the R hip is in contact with the floor. Focus of eyes is toward the legs. Return to Starting Position on Cts 5-6, and proceed to twist to left with similar angled thrust of legs and arms on Cts 7-8.

Note: Throughout the exercise, make sure that the legs do not touch the floor in the extended positions, and that the back straightens as much as possible.

Suggested Repetition: With practice, a total of 4 sets of 8 Counts each should be achieved before relaxing into a forward drop over the legs with the knees opening sideways.

33. TORSO TWIST II

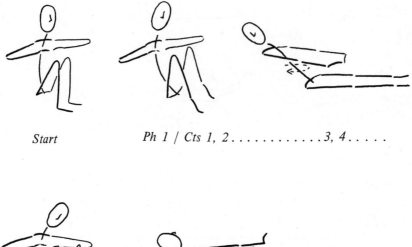

Start   *Ph 1 / Cts 1, 2 . . . . .3, 4 . . . . .*

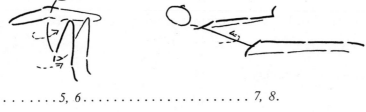

. . . . . . .5, 6 . . . . 7, 8.

34. TORSO TWIST III

A preparatory stretch for spiral body motions.

Count: Four phrases of 4 beats each.

Tempo: 52   *Music Quality:* Flowing, unaccented.

Starting Position: Sitting on the floor, R leg crossed over L knee which is bent at an acute angle on the floor with the foot tucked as close to the body as possible. R knee is in an upright position, both buttocks providing the base of body support. Arms at sides, hands lightly touching the floor.

Phrase 1: Bring L arm across R knee so that L elbow lies along the outside of R knee with forearm facing out and hand falling downward without stiffness. The palm faces out naturally, and the elbow against the knee creates a pressure point from which the body can twist. R shoulder now pulls back and the torso twists toward the right in a quarter-turn position (Cts 1-4). The head is turned as far to the right as possible with the eyes looking over the R shoulder to the rear of the room.

Phrase 2: With 4 soft, pulsating motions, twist the shoulders farther to the right, keeping the head in the turned position (Cts 5-8).

Phrase 3: Slowly change body position (Cts 1-4) without changing legs, and twist shoulders and head in the opposite direction (to the left) by bringing R arm over and across R knee and placing R elbow against R knee in angled position. R forearm aligns with inner side of R knee and foreleg, and hand grips ankle, making a firmly compact position which acts as a pressure point against which the torso twists.

Phrase 4: With 4 soft, pulsating motions, twist shoulders farther to the left, keeping head in turned position looking backward over L shoulder (Cts 5-8).

Repeat at least once, and then change legs, reversing all directions.

34. TORSO TWIST III

Pulsating twist of shoulders to right.

(seen from right side)

Start   *Ph 1/Cts 1-4. Ph 2/5-8.*

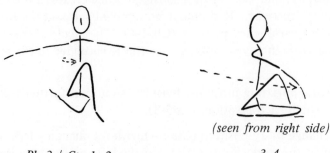

(seen from right side)

Ph 3 / Cts 1, 2 . . . . 3, 4.

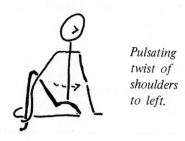

*Pulsating
twist of
shoulders
to left.*

(seen from left side)

Ph 4 / 1-4.

35. STOMACH AND BACK STRETCH

A backward and forward opening motion of the entire body in which the pelvis acts as a fulcrum. A total stretch followed by a closing motion in which arms and legs return to parallel position.

Count: Two phrases of 8 beats each.

Tempo and *Music Quality:* Same as above.

Starting Position: Use the double-leg extension position achieved at the end of Exercise 26.

Phrase 1: Begin to lower both legs slowly (Cts 1-4), tilting the torso farther back until it is almost horizontal with the floor (arms still extended sideways). The hips remain the fulcrum. The pull of the legs forward is balanced by the backward pull of the body, so that an outstretched position is achieved through muscle tension in the stomach and torso. As the legs near the floor (Ct 5), the torso begins to recover with an intake of breath and lift of the arms, the head falling backward. Continue the upward pull and return to the Starting Position, arms now overhead (Cts 5-8). The legs do not actually touch the floor until Ct 8.

Phrase 2: When the arms have passed vertically over the topmost point, the body begins to fall forward and subsequently bounces 4 times over the legs which remain straight, toes pointed, arms falling forward (Cts 1-4). Now the body pulls up again with curved back, regaining the Starting Position with the knees bending and straightening in the air (Cts 5-8). To achieve the return to this position, the arms must pull backward, curving with the body, and then stretch out sideways to reestablish the torso tilt and support.

Note: It is to be remembered that upward motions follow the pattern of the Recovery principle (slowing the tempo as the body reaches verticality); the reverse timing is true in the Falling motions.

Suggested Repetition: A total of 4 times for the complete exercise (16 beats).

35. STOMACH AND BACK STRETCH

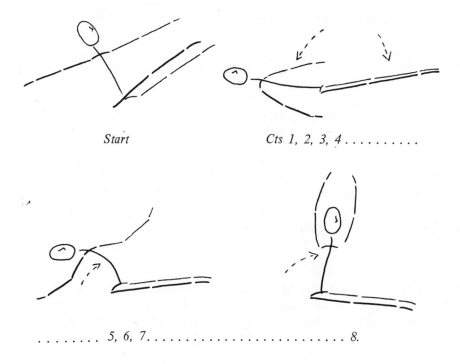

Start   *Cts 1, 2, 3, 4 . . . .*

. . . . *5, 6, 7 . . . . 8.*

Fall over: Ct 1, Bounce: 2, 3, 4 . . . 5, 6 . . . . 7 . . . . . . 8.

EXERCISE-STUDIES

36. DIAGONALS WITH TRANSITION

An Exercise-Study designed to stretch and strengthen the thighs and upper torso.

Count: Twelve phrases of 4 beats each on each side, plus 2-Count preparation and 8-Count transition (total 106 beats). Count in 8s.

Tempo: 42   *Music Quality:* Slow, flowing.

Starting Position: Assume a sitting position with the body turned to the downstage-right corner of the room, L leg bent away from the pelvis at a 60-degree (or more) angle with the L foot behind the knee, and close to the L buttock. R leg is extended, knee straight, toes pointed. The body position is on a diagonal, and the arms are alongside the hips, fingers lightly touching the floor. Head and eyes face the corner at eye level.

Preparation: Arms lift forward in parallel lines over the extended R leg. Hands and fingers maintain the straight line of the arms with the thumbs dropping easily in front of the palms. Body also lifts, without strain, as breath is inhaled (Cts 1-2).

Phrase 1: Stretching forward with the arms from the waist, keeping the hips on the floor and back leg in position, bend slowly over the outstretched R leg with rounded back (Cts 1-4). By Ct 4, the head is touching the R knee and the hands have reached the floor beyond the foot in long, softly extended lines; breath has been exhaled.

Phrase 2: Pulling upward and backward with rounded back, inhale and slowly recover to the Starting Position, letting the arms fall alongside the hips as the body lifts (Cts 5-8). The fingers have trailed along the floor and are now turning out, pointing backward, ready to carry the weight of the body on the sides of the hands[1] as they slide on the floor. The head is beginning to turn left in anticipation of the falling motion.

Phrase 3: Letting the weight of the body slide backward on the hands, slowly lower the torso with slightly arched back and head falling sideways toward the left (Cts 1-4). Slow exhalation. During this phrase, the R leg remains outstretched, and a true diagonal line is achieved through the body as it comes to a complete rest on the floor with the arms spread wing-like.

Phrase 4: With intake of breath, lift the torso, letting the head fall backward, and slowly recover to the Starting Position with the arms gradually reassuming their position at the sides of the body (Cts 5-8). The hands are now ready to reach forward, absorbing the original Preparation into the first forward stretch without extra counts.

Repeat these four phrases for a total of three times. On the third repeat, in pulling backward, keep the L arm forward in position as the body falls, and slide only on the R hand and arm. The recovery (Phrase 4) maintains the same positioning of the L arm, with the R arm gradually returning to the forward position. Head does not fall left, but pulls straight back with focus on L hand.

Transition: Right to Left

Keeping within the rhythmic phrase of 8 beats, bend the R knee out by folding the foot in, and let the arms fall to the sides (Ct 1). Dropping the body and head in an over-curve toward the R, pull the L leg forward through the knee while keeping the weight on the R buttock (Ct 2). With the L foot cleared from the floor, straighten it toward the right in preparation for a high circular motion from right to center-front (Cts 3-4). During this action, the arms coordinate by lifting forward and up with the body as it lifts, and the R knee simultaneously assumes a frontal knee-bent position with the foot on the floor (Cts 3-4). At this midpoint of the turn, the L leg is extended straight upward in front of the body, and the arms are curved convexly overhead with firm torso support. The turning movement continuing (Cts 5-6), the R knee begins to bend inward and the L leg begins to descend toward the left downstage corner while the arms are opening sideways and the body is turning to face toward the downstage-left corner of the room, thus completing the circular transitional motion. As the weight falls on the L leg and buttock, the R knee is free to maneuver and it turns outward toward a 60- (or more) degree angle; the entire body arrives at the diagonal position with the arms falling to the sides (Cts 7-8).

---

[1] This use of the "karate" edge of the hands—the outside surface—is a basic maneuver in almost every Humphrey fall.

Repeat the Diagonal sequence in its entirety twice; on the third backwards stretch (with the R arm forward in opposition to the L leg) there should be a musical and movement retard on Phrase 4, as the body slowly lifts back into position.

Exercise 36 Diagonals with Transition (Phrase 4, Count 6): Gail Corbin

36. DIAGONALS WITH TRANSITION

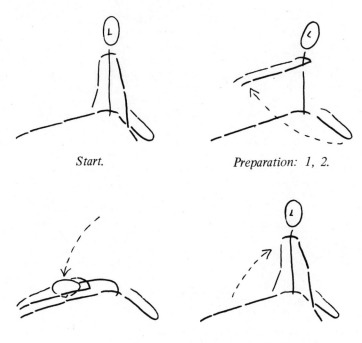

Start.   *Preparation: 1, 2.*

Ph 1 / Cts 1-4. . . . . *Ph 2 / Cts 5-8.*

Ph 3 / Cts 1 . . . . *3, 4.* . . . .

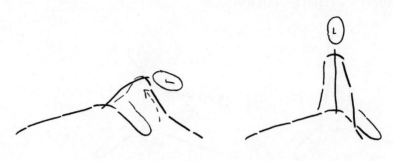

Ph 4 / Counts 5,6 · *7, 8.*

Repeat 2 times.   On 3rd repeat, left arm stays forward on pull back . . .

. . . . and on recovery.

Transition:

Ct 1 . . . . 2 . . . .

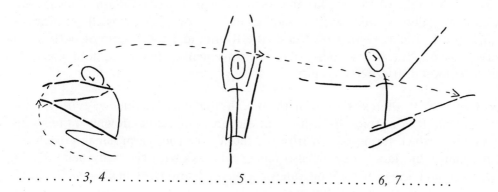

. . . . 3, 4 . . . . 5 . . . . 6, 7 . . . .

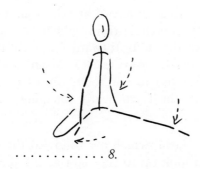

. . . . 8.

37. NINE-COUNT REBOUND STRETCHES WITH SUCCESSIONAL ARM LIFTS

An Exercise-Study designed to train the arms in successional movement while stretching legs and torso.

Count: One phrase consists of 3 measures of 3 beats each (9 beats); with an additional 6-beat preparation.

Tempo: 69   *Music Quality:* Lyrical in mood, sustained, flowing.

Starting Position: Facing front, legs stretched far apart as in Exercises 28-29; knees straight, toes pointed, body lifted, arms parallel to legs with palms facing front, fingers extended without strain, thumbs dropped in front of palms. Head and eyes focused forward.

Preparation: Maintaining leg and back positions, swing the arms downward, crossing them in front of the body with slight inward pressure of wrists and palms (Cts 1-3). With intake of breath, lift the torso, bringing the crossed arms upward successionally (elbows, then wrists, leading) into an overhead crossed position, in which the L arm is resting on top of the R arm, and the fingers of both hands curve over opposite elbows (Cts 4-6). The placement of the torso, head, and arms has a sculptural, frieze-like quality.

Measure 1: With the exhalation of the breath, the body falls sideways toward the R leg as the R arm, freed from its overhead position, swings downward in a sideways curve which terminates in front of the torso. The L arm remains overhead, still framing the face, but now also falling sideways with the body bend (Ct 1). The torso and arms form a long, sideways curve—L arm stretched above the head, R arm low across the waist. Rebound in this position in two soft bounces, breathing naturally (Cts 2-3).

Measure 2: On Ct 4, with fresh intake of breath, begin to swing the L arm far forward in a low horizontal semi-circle from right to left about 5″ above the floor. This movement will take the body forward also until the L hand comes to rest briefly on the instep of the L foot (Cts 5-6). Meanwhile, the R arm has stayed in the under-curve position close to the body. By Ct 6, the torso is bending sideways to the far left with the L ear nearly touching the L knee. Breath is now exhaled.

Measure 3: On Ct 7, the head, which has followed the movement leftward, now shifts focus and turns to look up to the right as the R arm starts to lift sideways successionally, pulling the body with it. Breath is inhaled as this movement occurs (Cts 7-9). In stretching upward on the right, the torso simultaneously frees the L arm from its outstretched position across the L leg, and it now pulls inward across the body's center, wrist and palm pressing first. This double-arm action brings the body to a peak position with the R arm high, the body supporting it, and the L arm in a reverse curve across the waist (Ct 9). Now the R arm is ready to fall with the body to the left and repeat the entire 9-Count phrase on the other side.

Suggested Repetition: 4 or more complete sequences (right and left), and a Conclusion.

Conclusion: Following the last successional upward lift of the L arm, bring that arm down slowly to shoulder height, opening wide to the side with elbow and wrist smoothly pulling outward and downward (Cts 1-3). The body has straightened to center position, and both arms are now extended evenly to the sides at shoulder height, the R arm having pulled outward in succession from its position across the waist as the body recovered. Repeat the preparatory motion of crossing both arms downward (Cts 4-6), and then, with a musical retard, slowly lift them into the overhead crossed position on the final 3 beats (Cts 7-9).

Variation: Twist and Rebound.

Count: Same as above.

Starting Position: Same as end of the Conclusion, above.

Measure 1: Twist the torso from the waist to the right (making sure that the pelvis stays grounded), dropping side-back in a quarter-turn twist over the L leg (similar to the Twist Variation, Exercise 14). The arms have opened to shoulder height in a wide curve and the breath is exhaled (Ct 1). Bounce softly backward in this position (Cts 2-3).

Measure 2: With intake of breath, flex both feet and swing the torso and arms counter-clockwise. The movement is initiated by pulling the R shoulder from its rear position toward the front (Ct 4). As the R arm reaches forward in the direction of the L leg, the L arm holds above the leg (Ct 5). Both hands meet, crossing at the wrists, and lightly touch the L ankle. Breath is expelled as the face falls over the L knee (Ct 6).

Measure 3: Now the body is facing the downstage-left corner of the room, except for the R leg which is still extended to its own side and pointed to the opposite downstage corner. With intake of breath on Ct 7, point toes again and lift the torso upward with arms rising in a successional curve to an overhead position in which the body line is straightened, the head and eyes looking toward the downstage-left corner of the room (Cts 8-9).

Repeat by alternating directions: drop from this peak position into a side-back fall to the right, and proceed with the bounces, the double action of the arms, etc.

37. NINE-COUNT REBOUND STRETCHES WITH SUCCESSIONAL ARM LIFTS

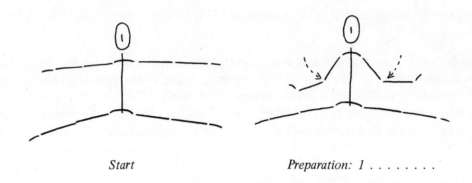

Start   *Preparation: 1* . . . .

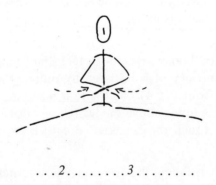

. . . *2* . . . . *3* . . . .

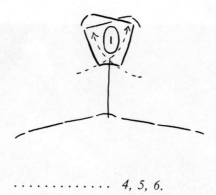

. . . . *4, 5, 6.*

Ct 1; Rebound: 2, 3 . . . . *4* . . . .

Exercise 37 Nine Count Rebound Stretches (Measure 3, Count 9): Gail Corbin

Exercise 37 Nine Count Rebound Stretches, Repetition to Left (Measure 1, Count 2-3): Gail Corbin

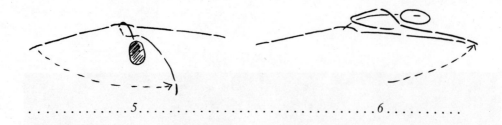

. . . . 5 . . . . 6 . . . .

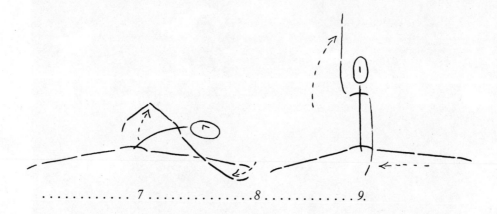

. . . . 7 . . . . 8 . . . . 9.

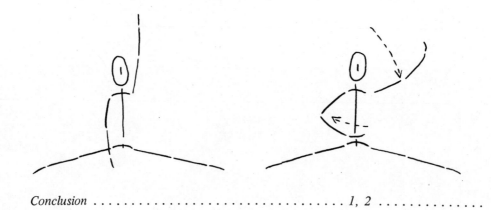

Conclusion . . . . *1, 2* . . . .

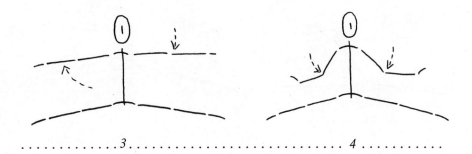

. . . . .3. . . . . 4 . . . .

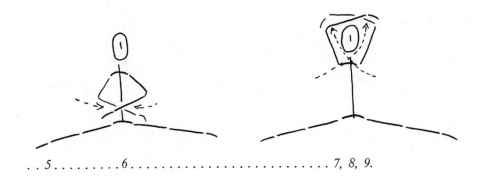

. . 5 . . . . .6. . . . . 7, 8, 9.

Variation: Twist and Rebound

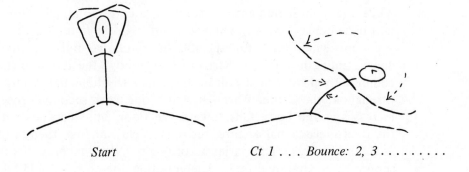

Start   Ct 1 . . . Bounce: 2, 3 . . . .

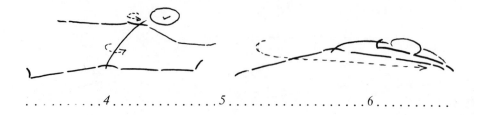

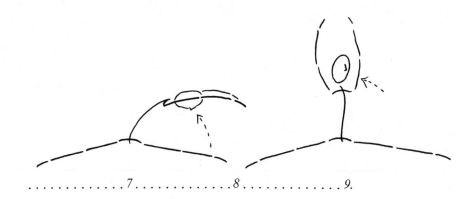

FIRST SERIES OF FALLS

These early Humphrey Falls use Successional Movement in general for both the descent and the ascent; the Fall and Recovery are achieved through naturally related body parts used sequentially. While the main ingredient is *relaxation,* a correspondingly important ingredient is *control,* which is manifest in the *timing.*

Except when used for specific interpretative purposes in a dance, timing in the First Series of Falls follows the action of succumbing to gravitational pull in the general rhythmic pattern used throughout the Center Warm-Up and Floor Work sections: speed increases as the body falls toward the floor, but decreases with the final successional gesture; recovery is slow at first, then faster as the body rises. This varies according to individual muscular response to gravitational pull. The counting, therefore, should take into consideration the acceleration or deceleration occurring between the counts, which only indicate areas of action rather than exact placement at a given instant.

Beginning with the Falls, instructions regarding the use of breath exhalation on downward motions and inhalation on rising ones will be omitted, presuming that the teacher and the student now understand the principles of breath-and-body coordinations and will incorporate them whenever possible.

38. BACK FALL

Count: A preparation and two phrases of approximately 6 beats each.

Tempo: Ad lib (according to the teacher's use of instructional material). *Suggested Accompaniment:* Timed chords, drum, and/or gong. For the Preparation, a rush of fast drumbeats starting softly and becoming increasingly louder. A pause and, as the body falls, one fairly loud gong stroke. If the sequence ends with the first recovery, a diminuendo rush of drumbeats might be given. Or, if Falls continue, one might repeat the same beats as for the Preparation, etc.

Starting Position: Facing front, feet in parallel position, arms relaxed at sides.

Preparation: A vertical lift through the body before falling. Beginning with an impulse in the knees, draw the arms forward and upward successively with the body and head lifting simultaneously. Rise to full height on the half-toes, with the back arching slightly and the hips well forward. Tension gathers visibly. The body is on the verge of falling forward as a result of the continued arching and backward pull of the arms and head, which is now dropping back. There is a moment of total suspension.

Phrase 1: Fall. Losing control, the body falls forward with the R foot catching the weight in a deep forward lunge that stretches the body its full length (R knee bends completely, heel off the floor, L leg is taut, heel off the floor). Hands strike the floor and the head curves over the knee (Cts 1-2). Immediately draw the L leg behind the R leg (Ct 3), bending the L knee to its side at a 90-degree angle (if possible), making sure that the L foot remains relaxed so that it will not interfere with the placement of the buttocks on the floor behind it. This occurs as the body sits briefly on the floor and then begins to unfold backward as the hands slide along the floor on either side (Ct 4). In this movement, the hands and hips are catching the body's weight, with the L leg folded underneath; the final unrolling of the back and straightening of the front (R) leg take place as the hands steer backward opening wing-like on the floor (Cts 5-6).

Phrase 2: Recovery. Lift the torso through the rib cage, as in Phrase 4 of Exercise 36, letting the head fall backward and the arms trail behind (Cts 1-2). Once the body has risen to a near-sitting position, draw the R knee up (foot on floor), and with hands still behind hips, drop the body forward and over (Cts 3-4).

Now the motion gathers momentum; pushing off the floor, transfer weight from the L knee to the R foot, continuing to rise (Ct 5) until the Starting Position is achieved (Ct 6).

Alternate Recovery. At this point, the recovery can terminate in a final stance in which the arms are raised successively above the head with a corresponding lift of the body by the end of Ct 6; or, having achieved this upward lift, the Fall can be repeated from this position with a further arching of the back, a L foot forward lunge, and a R leg backward bend.

38. BACK FALL

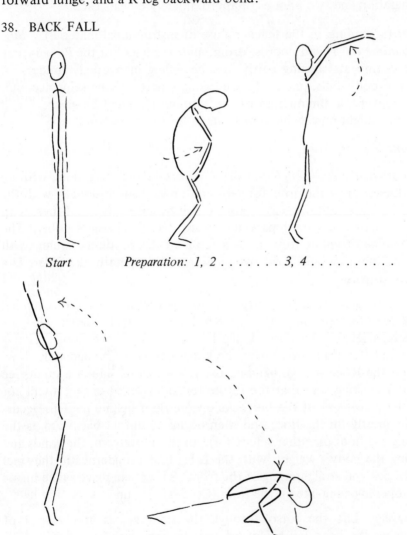

Start   Preparation: 1, 2 . . . . 3, 4 . . . .

. . . . .5, 6.   Ph 1 / Cts 1, 2 . . . .

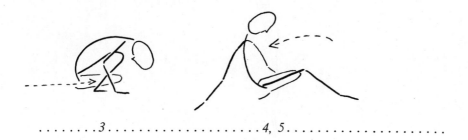

. . . . *3* . . . . *4, 5* . . . .

. . . . *6.*   *Ph 2 / Cts 1, 2* . . . . .

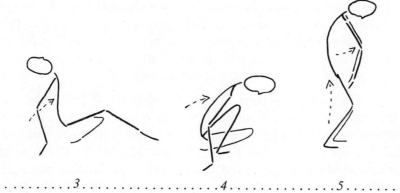

. . . . *3* . . . . *4* . . . . *5* . . . .

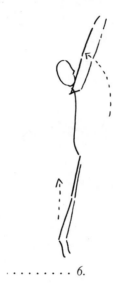

. . . . 6.

39. SIDE FALL

Count: Two phrases of approximately 4 slow beats each.

Tempo: Ad lib (according to the teacher's use of instructional material). ***Suggested Accompaniment:*** Timed chords, drum, and/or gong.

Starting Position: Facing front, feet parallel, hands at sides.

Preparation: Fall to the Right. Looking to the right, step sideways to the left on the L foot with knee bent for impulse, and swing the R arm to the right in an undercurve, palm up, with the fingers leading, as if beckoning someone (Ct 1). Continuing the motion of the R arm upward and above the head, pull the R leg alongside the L leg to the extreme left, making a long high curve from the ankles, which are now together, to the fingertips of the R hand (Ct 2). R arm continues to pull overhead to the left, causing the body to continue stretching in that direction. Breath is suspended, and the body's weight is principally carried on the L foot with the R foot ready to leave the floor. L arm remains in outwardly curved position close to L side throughout the above action.

Phrase 1: Fall. Releasing the pent-up energy, swing the R arm down across the front of the body while still bending to the far left. At this point, the L knee bends further allowing the R knee to drop to the floor with the foot placed directly behind it (do not curl toes but keep them relaxed). As the R arm passes from left to right across the knees, (Ct 2-"and"), the pelvis—now lowered to a near-sitting position—is skimming to the right over the upturned R heel (Ct 3). Momentum gathering, the energy is completely released as the R hip slides to the floor, the R hand, quickly descending to catch the body's weight, stretches out in advance of the falling torso, and the extended fingers slide the body to the floor (Ct 4).

Final Position. Body prone on its side (R), L arm in front of body, hand on floor, R knee still bent, L leg extended over it (make sure that it does not bounce up on final motion), R arm extended in a straight line to the R with the head lying on the R shoulder. The whole body now forms a straight line.

Phrase 2: Recovery. Drawing the body up successively to the left (torso and L arm pulling sideways with head still dropped to the right and R arm still low), come to a semi-sitting position with the hips skimming back over the still-overturned R foot (Cts 1-2). Transfer the weight without pause to the L leg, which has been gradually bending during the above procedure, and step sideways onto the L foot while swinging both arms to the left (Ct 3). The swing of the arms enables the body to rise smoothly in an under-curve pattern, pulling the R leg through the hip. With the weight transferred to the L leg, the body rises and the R arm continues the circle (the L arm stays at its side) coming to high above the head by the end of Ct 3. At this point, the body has reached a full standing position, feet together, and is facing front (Ct 3-"and"). On Ct 4, the R arm descends in a wide curve to its side.

Repeat, reversing directions for a Side Fall to the left.

39. SIDE FALL

Start　　　*Preparation: 1* . . . . . .　. . . . . *2.*

Ph 1 / Ct . . . . *2 and* . . . . *3* . . . .

. . . . *4.*

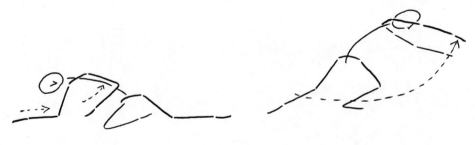

Ph 2 / Recovery: Ct 1 . . . . *2* . . . . *3* . . . .

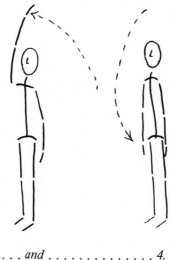

. . . and . . . . 4.

40. FRONT FALL

Count: Two phrases of approximately 4 beats each.

Tempo: Ad lib (according to the teacher's use of instructional material). **Suggested Accompaniment:** Timed chords, drum, and/or gong.

Starting Position: Facing diagonally downstage-left corner of the room and allowing plenty of space ahead, place weight on L foot with R foot on poised half-toe close to the L ankle. Both arms hang loosely at the side. Focus of eyes toward left corner.

Phrase 1: Fall, including a preparatory oppositional swing with a hop. Count "and" for an impulse, and then step forward on the R foot taking a traveling hop while swinging the L leg forward to hip height with the knee slightly bent at an angle of about 45 degrees; the L arm, coordinating with the L leg, swings forward and upward to a vertical position above the shoulder; the R arm stays alongside the body (Ct 1). As the L foot lands in front of the body (about 18″), the knee bends forward with the body leaning forward over it. The momentum engendered by the hop carries the body's weight far ahead of the L knee (which does not touch the floor until the final position), and the L hand, having swung forward and down, is ready to catch the weight by sliding forward on the side of the hand (Ct 2). As the sliding begins, the R hand also comes into contact with the floor, and sharing the weight, enables the whole body to slide diagonally across the floor (Cts 3-4). The momentum of this falling motion produces a slide of at least 2 ½'.

Final Position: Body prone on the floor in the direction of the downstage-left corner of the room. Both legs are straight and together, L elbow bent and close to waist alongside the body, head turned to left, R arm straight and pointing ahead.

Phrase 2: *Recovery.* Pulling backward with rounded body and R arm bending close to side, palm down, place both knees on the floor, curl toes under, and shift weight as smoothly as possible from knees to soles of feet using hands lightly (Cts 1-2). As heels come to floor, rise to standing successively through body (Cts 3-4). The recovery completed, turn to face the downstage-right corner of the room in readiness to repeat the Front Fall in the other direction with the hop-step on the L foot and the R arm coordinating with R leg as it swings forward.

40. FRONT FALL

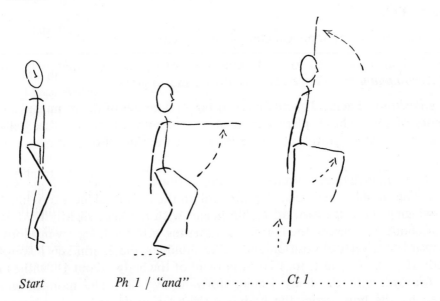

Start   Ph 1 / "and" · · · · · · · · · · · · Ct 1 · · · · · · · · · · · · · ·

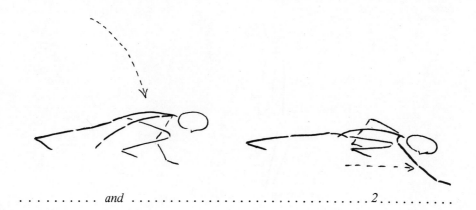

. . . . *and* . . . . .2. . . . .

. . . . .3. . . . . 4 *(final position).*

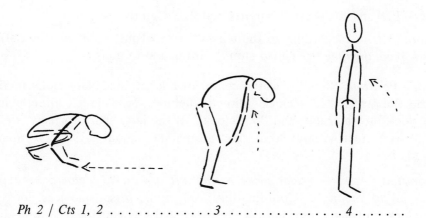

Ph 2 / Cts 1, 2 . . . . .3. . . . . .4. . . . . . .

.... *ready for other side.*

41. CIRCULAR FALL

This Fall, sometimes called "Spiral," conveys the dynamic image of a whirlpool. Once started in its downward spiraling, it pulls faster and faster around an imaginary center.

    The analysis below should encourage the student to follow instructions as if relating the changing positions to an imaginary clock placed on the floor. When the circular fall is understood and mastered, the momentum of the movement will naturally swing the body around farther than indicated with these directions. Analyzed in detail, this fall seems very complex, but once the primary leg action is achieved (Cts 1-2), the remaining motions follow quite easily, if the student keeps in mind the image of a descending spiral.

Count: Fall and Recovery of approximately 9 Counts each.

Tempo: Ad lib (according to the teacher's use of instructional material). *Suggested Accompaniment:* Timed chords, drum, and/or gong.

Starting Position: Standing in the center of a large, imaginary clock marked out on the floor with "12 o'clock" directly behind, "6 o'clock" directly in front, "9 o'clock" to the right, and "3 o'clock" to the left. Turn to face "7 o'clock." The torso is erect without strain, feet are parallel, about 1 ½" to 2" apart, arms relaxed at sides.

Preparation: A semi-circular swing to the left toward "3 o'clock" in preparation for a fall to the right. Coordinating head, arms, torso, and legs, look toward "3 o'clock," lifting arms sideways chest-high and swinging them counter-clockwise with the torso while stepping out on the L foot in the same direction. This movement is circular insofar as the entire body pivots to the left on the R foot, which remains in place. The distance between the feet should be approximately a full leg's length: the R leg behind the body, turned out from the hip and its heel pulled from the floor. The L leg, now carrying the body's weight, has the knee well bent, turned out over the foot and the heel on the floor. Arms are still open sideways.

Fall. Clockwise Direction

Counts 1-2: With a quick turn of the head to the right, anticipating a change of weight from the L leg to the R leg, swing shoulders, torso, and hips toward "7 o'clock" while peripherally reaching out clockwise with the arms from the waist (Ct 1). To accomplish this, the R leg pivots from the stretched preparatory position to a turned-out, heel-down placement with the knee bent facing "8 o'clock." The body's weight is now over the R leg. Simultaneously, the L leg is turned out and momentarily straightened with the heel lifted from the floor. The preparatory stretch has reversed itself. Moreover, a descent has been indicated in the somewhat deeper bend of the R knee and commensurate lowering of the body in the direction of the spiral. All of this occurs on Ct 1. Continuing the motion of turning and descending, the L foot slides behind the R leg until the L foot, relaxed and on its side, is ready to touch the floor; meanwhile, the bent L knee has passed behind the deeper-bending R knee and is emerging to the right of it. The arms, still describing the peripheral pull, have brought the torso around toward "11 o'clock." These maneuvers are completed by Ct 2, and the body is at half-height.

Counts 3-4: With the downward pull increased in volume, the buttocks and the sides of the L knee and foot touch the floor in a cross-legged sitting position with the arms still stretched forward peripherally and pulling the body past the R knee in a clockwise descent (Ct 3). At this point, the R knee is still flexed upward with the heel on the floor, and the arms are passing through "1 o'clock." With the torso pulling more emphatically to the right, the R knee falls sideways in the same direction, and in doing so, frees the L knee to align itself alongside on a downward slant. The R hand is now just touching the floor and the L hand, still outstretched, is pointing to "2 o'clock" (Ct 4).

Counts 5-6: Catching the body's weight on the side of the R hand, slide on the R side of the torso and hips in a sweeping clockwise curve while passing through "5 o'clock." Both legs fall sideways—knees bent, the R leg under and farther forward than the L leg. The toes are pointing backward toward "9 o'clock." The L arm is now pointing toward "6 o'clock" and then moving parallel to the R arm which has slid all the way to the floor (Ct 5). Immediately, the hips slide forward to form an arc with the torso, so that the body appears to be opening outward resting sideways on the hips and R shoulder in the descending pattern of the spiral. The increased pull has brought the L arm over the head, pulling it backward toward "11 o'clock," with the arching of the torso (Ct 6).

Counts 7-8-9: The energy waning, the movement begins to slow down. The L shoulder now touches the floor, and the R arm starts to curve overhead pulling the torso more and more to the left while the hips remain tautly curved to the right (Cts 7-8). The hands in parallel are pointing toward "2 o'clock" on the floor. With a final gesture of relaxation, the body rests in this position for Ct 9, having made nearly two 360-degree turns in its descent from the preparatory position.

Recovery

Counts 1-2: Reversing the movement in form and speed, pull the body to the right, sliding the R elbow inward under the R side. The R hand should be facing the floor and the forearm carrying part of the torso's weight as the R shoulder is pulled off the floor. The L arm is circling back over the head at the same time, pointing from "2 o'clock" back through "12 o'clock," and the hips have relaxed from their forward thrust (Ct 1). The arms, legs, and body are now retracing the circular path of the fall, pulling up with increasing speed. As the recovery goes into Ct 2, the knees, still lying sideways on the floor, bend farther toward the R hip (also still on the floor), while the back, no longer arching, is rounding over and beginning to pull in the direction of the counter-clockwise ascent. At this point, the emphasis is on the L arm movement, which is reaching out as far as possible toward "9 o'clock." The body's weight is now on the R elbow, the head looking toward the fingers of the L hand (Ct 2).

Counts 3-4: Continuing the ascent with increased speed, keep reaching peripherally counter-clockwise (with both arms now), passing from "9 o'clock" backward through "7 o'clock," and bring both knees into a loosely-held upright parallel position (Ct 3). With the spiral pull continuing toward the left with increased energy, drop the L knee to the left, releasing the foot, and cross the R knee over it, placing the R foot squarely on the floor next to the L thigh. The body is now facing "5 o'clock," but the arms, still parallel, are moving ahead toward "4 o'clock" and slanting leftward as the L shoulder pulls more. The R shoulder is now higher than the L, and the momentum is steadily increasing.

Counts 5-6: Placing the weight on the R foot, start to rise, turning from "4 o'clock" through "2 o'clock," all the while pulling through the body, head, and arms to the left in counter-clockwise motion (Ct 5). The movement continuing, the body is now almost upright with the arms higher than the head but still "bank-ing" leftward to pull into a spin (Ct 6). You are passing "12 o'clock" at least.

Counts 7-8-9: With increased momentum, start spinning to the left, feet closing together on the half-toe, both arms still pulling side-back (counter-clockwise) from the waist, but rising higher as they do so. The spin continuing, the out-stretched arms spiral upward faster and faster until the circling closes in at the top with the body completely straightened after having coordinated with the arm pull in the final ascent (Cts 7-8). The momentum reaching a climax, the spin stops on Ct 9 with the body facing front ("6 o'clock") and pulled upward. The feet are together on half-toe, the head is lifted, the eyes looking past the hands, which are still parallel but stretched directly above the shoulders.

Repeat in the opposite direction: counter-clockwise for the descent; clockwise for the recovery.

41. CIRCULAR FALL

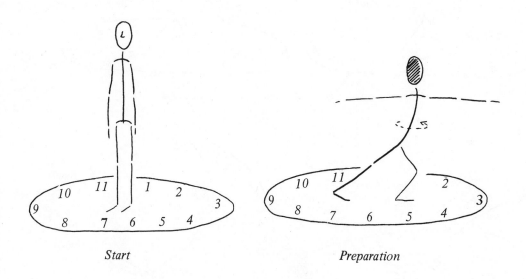

Start   *Preparation*

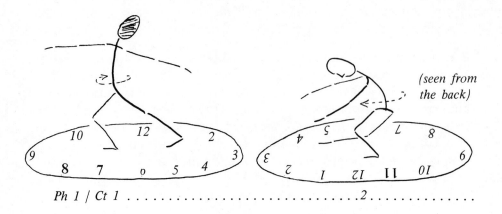

Ph 1 / Ct 1 . . . . .2 . . . .

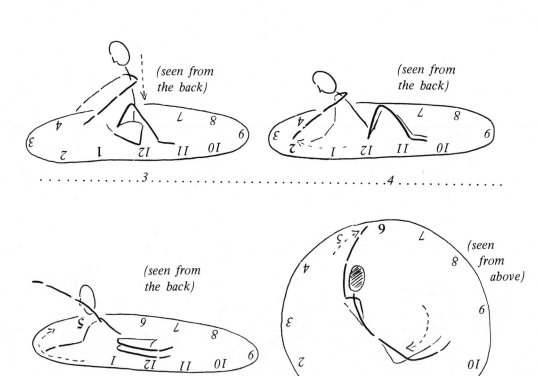

. . . . .3 . . . . .4 . . . .

. . . . .5 . . . .

(seen from the back)

(seen from the back)

(seen from the back)

(seen from the back)

(seen from above)

(seen from the front)

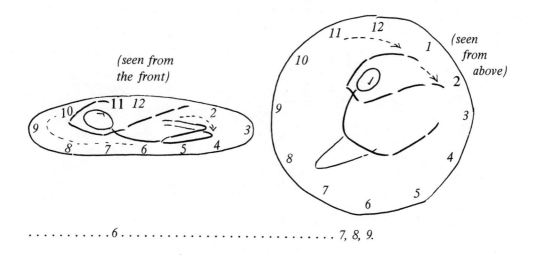

(seen from above)

. . . . *6* . . . . *7, 8, 9.*

(seen from above)

(seen from the front)

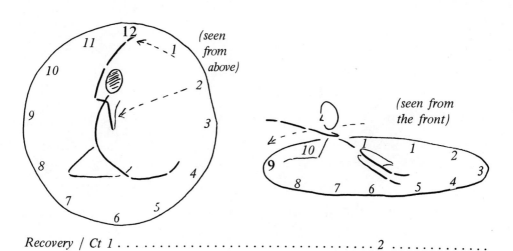

Recovery | Ct 1 . . . . *2* . . . .

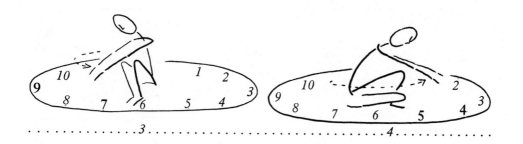

. . . . *3* . . . . *4* . . . .

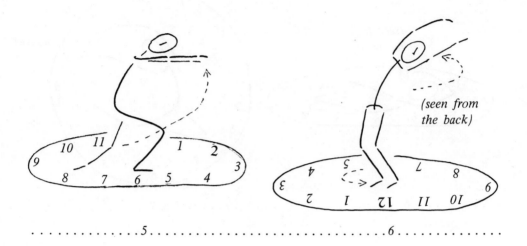

(seen from the back)

. . . . .5. . . . . .6. . . . .

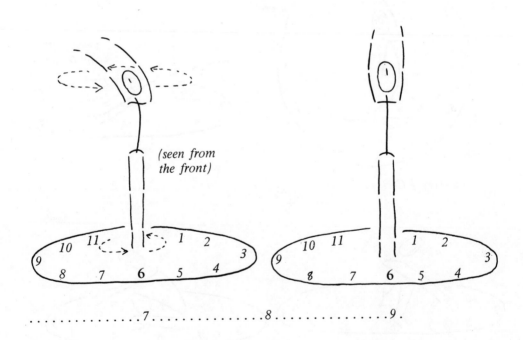

(seen from the front)

. . . . .7. . . . . .8. . . . . .9.

EXERCISE-STUDY

42. TWENTY-FOUR COUNT STUDY

An Exercise-Study aimed to develop fluency of phrasing in a rhythmically-related series of rising and falling motions.

Count: Six phrases of 4 beats each, counting 1-24.

Tempo: 52   *Music Quality:* Lyrical, flowing, coming to a climax at the end of Phrase 5 with a retard and resolution on Phrase 6.

Starting Position: Facing front, midstage, heels together, toes turned out not more than 30 degrees. Arms at sides, slightly convex. Focus forward.

Phrase I: A descent in the form of a ceremonious bow.   Step back on L foot (same turn-out as above) with impulse in L knee to initiate a circular swinging movement of the R leg forward, up, and to the right side with a hip-high extension; the R arm, moving simultaneously with the leg, also lifts forward, then above the head and to the R side in similar rhythmic phrasing (Cts 1-2). The torso, in supporting this motion, lifts graciously and ceremoniously with the face expressively indicating the nature of the gesture.   On Ct 3, the R leg completes the circle backward and is crossing behind the standing leg with both knees turned out and bending, the R knee having passed the L leg to the far side of it.   In descending simultaneously with the R leg, the R arm has dropped to the right side, and the body is curving forward slightly in the descent which ends on Ct 4 in a sitting position.   The head, dropping forward, completes the bow as the body settles on the floor.   At the conclusion of Phrase 1, the L knee is directly in front of the chest, the foot flat on the floor, both arms forming convex curves with the fingertips touching the floor.

Phrase 2: A secondary circular bow.   Upon sitting, immediately release the L leg (Ct 5) by lifting it forward, straightening the knee, and simultaneously bring the L arm forward parallel to it, with the fingers softly extended.   The body and head are lifting up correspondingly in the same direction.   You are now sitting on the R hip, facing front, the fingers of the R hand still touching the floor with the arm in the sideways convex curve.   On Ct 6, circle the L leg to the left, lifting it higher as it moves sideways, and lift the L arm above the L shoulder, pulling the torso upward; continue the circular motion stretching the L leg and arm to the back, thus twisting the torso sideways to the left in preparation for the "secondary bow." This movement will bring the R shoulder, arm, and hand to the front in a counterclockwise curve.   In accomplishing this motion, the R hand skims the floor peripherally. By Ct 8, the body is dropping sideways on the R arm and shoulder with the R knee in a bent position on its side. The L leg is resting in a semi-bent position on the floor behind the elongated torso, and the L arm is parallel to it.

Phrase 3: A sideways extension with the L leg. Begin to pull sideways to the right, skimming the R hand back over the floor clockwise until it is about 14″ from the R hip. This movement brings the torso up to face front. Concurrently, the L leg is lifted off the floor, L arm parallel to it, and carried forward through the air, knee leading. The L arm remains parallel to the leg (Cts 9-10). Both hips are lifted by Ct 10 and the weight falls more and more on the side of the R knee and the R hand. The head has turned in the direction of the L leg and arm, and the back has straightened out. On Cts 11 and 12, the L leg is extending sideways from its knee-bent position to a full extension, turned out from the hip. The body is leaning to the far right with the hips still suspended in a frontal slant. By the end of Ct 12, the line of the body is one long, scooping curve from the outstretched L leg and arm down through the hips, and up again to the right through the torso and head. Head and eyes are still looking upward to the left.

Phrase 4: A high circular stretch of the L arm over the body from left to right, and return. With the L leg remaining in the sideways extension and turning out from the hip, the L arm starts to trace a high overhead curve toward the right; at the same time, the hips lift to support the motion. During this arching movement (Cts 13-14), the body's weight is shared by the R hand, as before, and by the R knee, now securely positioned under the R hip. Both hips have pulled up from the low scooping position to face front, and the face is turning toward the right, anticipating the arm's descent. On Ct 15, two actions coordinate to produce light-touch "rebound" motion: the L knee bends with the foot pointing directly behind the hip, and the torso and L arm drop sideways to the right with an accent which prepares for a retracing of the overhead curve. Immediately afterward, the face turns upward, the eyes following the motion of the ascent. By Ct 16, the L arm is being lowered (behind the L leg) to shoulder height, the hips drop back to the "scooped" position of Cts 11 and 12, and the L knee has again straightened into its former high extension; head now looks in direction of the extended L foot.

Phrase 5: A recovery to standing. From the high sideways extension of the L leg, begin to pull to the right with the torso (turning the head in that direction) while still holding the L arm in the position of Ct 16. In coordination with this pull, bring the L leg to the front in a clockwise motion, bending the knee up as it crosses in front of the body. This double action of torso and leg, while the L arm stays more or less fixed, enables the R knee and hand to share the body's

Exercise 42 Twenty-four Count Study (Phrase 3, Count 9): Margo Knis

Exercise 42 Twenty-four Count Study (Phrase 6, Count 24). Gail Corbin

support (Ct 17). Place the L foot completely on the floor—it should be turned out with the knee in line with the toes—and begin to transfer the body's weight from the R knee to the L foot. As the weight is being transferred, the L arm stabilizes the torso pull by holding its position, and the R arm assists in the shift by lifting sideways convexly. The body is thus pulled up, and the L thigh takes over the major effort of the recovery (Ct 18), during which the hips should remain under the shoulders. Immediately begin to turn to the right by pulling the R shoulder toward its own side, as in the Recovery of the Spiral Fall, thus enabling the body to rotate easily while rising. You are now on half-toe and pivoting to the right. During the turn to the back, the L arm remains at the body's side while the upward successional motion is carried mostly by the R arm; by Ct 19, when the body is almost attaining full height, the L arm is pulling up successionally also, and the spiral ascent is about to be concluded. On Ct 20, both arms are stretching upward to a parallel position overhead, and the body faces diagonally to "5 o'clock." In this stance, the hips are in line with the shoulders; the head is lifted in the direction of stage left; and the feet, on half-toe, are placed parallel, approximately 2" apart, with the L foot in advance of the R foot at a comfortable distance. This position should be secure for the descent (adjust distances according to leg and body proportions).

Phrase 6: A slow half-fall. On Ct 21, twist the shoulders farther to the right, without changing the angled placement of the legs and hips, and bend the knees bringing the heels off the floor. The upper body is now assuming a straight front position while the hips still face "5 o'clock." Looking upward toward the L hand, start a slow descent, in which the R arm circles sideways toward the floor, palm downward, stretching out and down with the torso (Ct 22). During this slow falling motion, the knees are bending more deeply and the L arm is beginning to bend from the elbow, the hand descending toward the L shoulder, palm down. The R hand is about to touch the floor to the side of the R shoulder, and the body has remained in a straight slanting line from the knees, never breaking at the hips (Ct 23). The knees are now fully bent and on the floor at an acute angle, the hips lifted and angled side-front (see Exercise 30 for strengthening preparation), the toes of both feet curled under; the R elbow, also on the floor by now, is in line with the R hand and supporting part of the body's weight (Ct 24). This movement completes the study.

Repeat the full twenty-four Counts with the R foot taking the initial step backward and the entire proceedings reversed.

42. TWENTY-FOUR COUNT STUDY

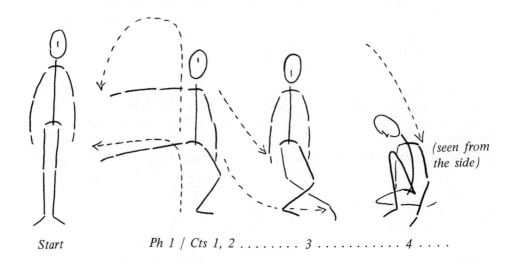

(seen from the side)

Start   *Ph 1 / Cts 1, 2 . . . . 3 . . . . 4 . . . .*

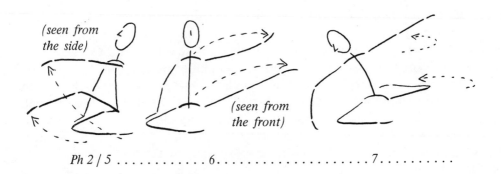

(seen from the side)

(seen from the front)

Ph 2 / 5 . . . . 6 . . . . 7 . . . .

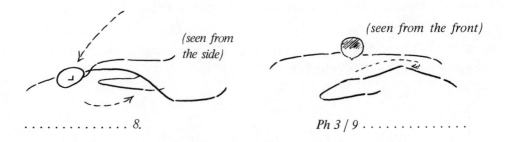

(seen from the side)

(seen from the front)

. . . . 8.   *Ph 3 / 9 . . . .*

. . . . *10.* . . . . *11* . . . .

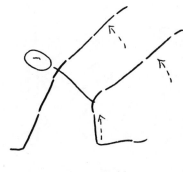

. . . . *12.*

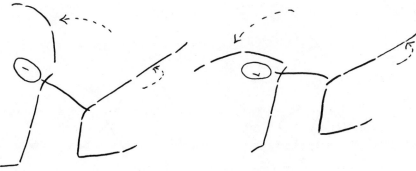

Ph 4 / 13 . . . . *14* . . . .

. . . .*15*. . . . .

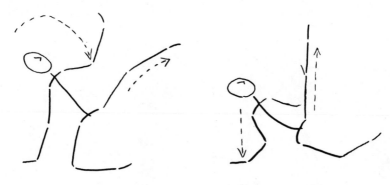

. . . .*16*. . . . .

. . . .*Ph 5 / 17* . . . .*18* . . . .

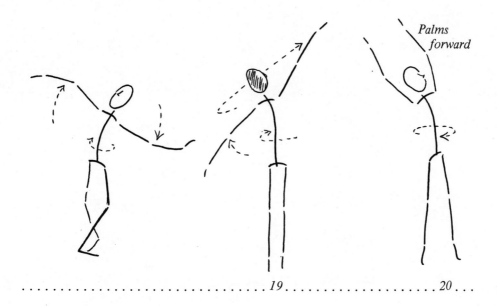

Palms forward

. . . . *19* . . . . *20* . . .

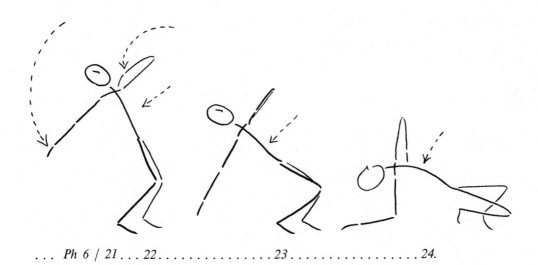

. . . *Ph 6 / 21* . . . *22* . . . . *23* . . . . *24.*

Chapter 5

BARRE WORK

INTRODUCTION

In the early days, we never used a barre. The search for fundamentals in natural movement led to other means of developing the body's technical resources. Besides, technique as an aim in itself was yet to become the modern dancer's goal. The main thing in those times was to discover how to express ideas and feelings through a movement vocabulary of one's own.

"Technique is specifically pointed toward saying something . . . not thought of first as [a] separate activity,"[1] wrote Doris Humphrey in a manuscript that bears no date, but is surely of the years when the search was most intense. Nevertheless, the Humphrey Technique evolved into specific forms as we have seen in Chapters 3 and 4. A style emerged as a result of exploring natural movement in all its phases; at the same time, technical skills inevitably developed. The skills we acquired could not possibly have approached those of today's modern dancers, but we never confused the "act" with the "aim." For this reason, the Humphrey Technique became both a unique style and a strenuous, demanding one.

However, as modern dancers were soon to recognize, the barre offers anchorage while the dancer works first one leg and then the

[1]Doris Humphrey Collection. Folder M-58.

other. The barre aligns the body with the structure of the building where the training takes place, instilling in the dancer's consciousness a parallel relationship of the spine to the wall as its vertical partner. Once modern dancers began to view technique as intrinsically efficient, as well as a means to an end, the barre began to have widespread use. For those Humphrey dancers who, like myself, had ballet training at an early age, it was natural to work at the barre, utilizing Doris's theories to their full extent.

Even in Doris's early classes, there was a facsimile of barre support in the "double successions": two dancers, facing each other and grasping right or left hands, would perform a circular succession, first each one alone and then in unison. That arm linkage produced the same anchorage a barre would. This was Doris Humphrey's imaginative way of solving the balance problem. Certain fundamental ballet procedures, such as the necessary turn-out of the leg from the hip joint, leg extensions, and the formal use of the arms in preparations, are incorporated into some of the following exercises and studies. However, the basic Humphrey feeling of "wholeness" should remain the dominant characteristic of all the movements.

SUCCESSIONAL STRETCHES

Use of the barre as an almost total weight-bearing support to enable the dancer to execute sideways, backward, and forward body stretches in continuous curves, both convex and concave.

Count: Phrases of 7s (8s acceptable as well) for all directions.

Tempo: 54   *Music Quality:* Sustained.

43. SIDEWAYS STRETCH

Starting Position: Feet parallel and together. Body placed directly over legs and a distance of nearly a full arm's length from the barre. L hand on barre. R arm relaxed at the side. Focus forward.

Phrase 1: (Cts 1-7 [8]). With an impulse in both knees start a successional movement from the ankles to the far right, allowing the knees—which are somewhat bent and still facing front—to fall toward the center of the room. There should be a strong pull outward through the hips as they carry the movement sideways and upward. As the succession from the ankles to the hips is taking place, the outside

Exercise 43 Successional Stretches, Sideways (Phrase 1, Count 7 or 8): Margo Knis

arm parallels the action, tracing a second curve far away from the body itself. At this point, the dancer is literally falling away from the barre with the inside arm (L) maintaining support. The motion continuing through the torso, the R arm stretches over the head, which has now dropped toward the barre in a tilted position. The completed sideways stretch makes a nearly elliptical design.

Phrase 2: With emphasis on the waist stretch and maintaining the curve, the knees still slightly bent, 7 (8) soft bounces in this extreme position. Hips must remain in the flat frontal position while the diaphragm and torso are visibly lifted in the body's sideways curve. Take care not to hunch the shoulders.

Phrase 3: (Cts 1-7 [8]). Reversing the stretch, retrace the sideways curve by first lifting upward, then outward and downward with the R arm describing the arc, while the body, after regaining its upright position when the arm is overhead, begins to fall toward the barre at hip-point; as the R arm stretches far to the right, the L hip is almost touching the wall, and the body's weight is about to fall inward in a concave sideways curve. As the inside fall takes place, the L arm bends with elbow and shoulder pulled up, head falling sideways-right. At this point, the R hand is placed on the R hipbone, elbow crooked.

Phrase 4: 7 (8) soft bounces in this extreme reverse curve toward the barre.

Repeat the entire exercise once or twice more. Then face the other direction and stretch with the L arm.

43. SIDEWAYS STRETCH

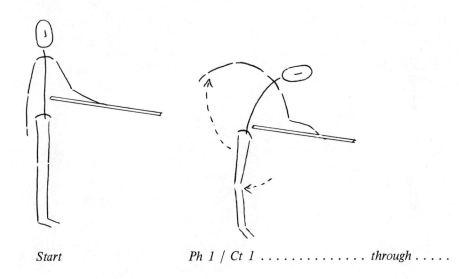

Start   *Ph 1 / Ct 1 . . . . through . . . . .*

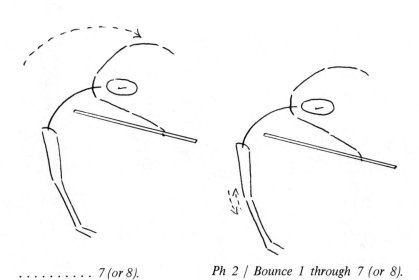

. . . . 7 (or 8).   *Ph 2 / Bounce 1 through 7 (or 8).*

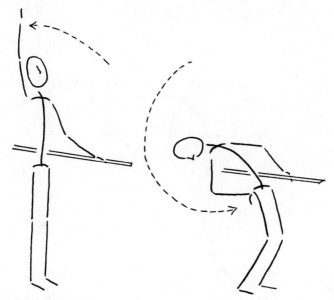

Ph 3 / Cts 1, 2, 3 . . . . 4, 5, 6, 7 (or 8).

Ph 4 / Bounce 1 through 7 (or 8).

44. BACKWARD STRETCH

Starting Position: Facing the barre at almost arm's length distance, both hands on barre; feet together.

Phrase 1: (Cts 1-7 [8]). Holding firmly, drop the torso forward and over, and simultaneously bend both knees toward the wall. From this position, begin a vertical succession through the hips, torso, neck, and head until the body is well arched (both hands still on the barre). The head falls back and the chest lifts at the highest point of the stretch. The feet (now on half-toe), legs, and pelvis are in a straight line, while the backward arching is clearly seen in the upper torso, neck, and head.

Phrase 2: (Cts 1-7 [8]). Reversing the stretch, hold the barre with both hands and pull backward with the hips, straighten the knees, and flatten the back so that the upper body is stretched in a horizontal plane, parallel to the floor. The design of the body is now an acute angle. The heels are on the floor and the head is dropped forward, not lower, however, than the arms as they are tautly stretched from the barre.

Phrase 3: (Cts 1-7 [8]). A repeat of Phrase 1 from the above position, which demands a deeper knee-bend impulse in order to transfer the weight inward toward the barre. But the procedure following this maneuver is the same; the succession is terminated in a high, backward arch of the upper torso.

Repeat once or twice more.

Variation: Starting from the end of Phrase 3, take one hand off the barre, describe a full circle with that arm by lifting it forward, up, and backward behind the body, and return it to the barre, cupping the fingers under the barre for support (Cts 1-4). As the hand catches the barre on Ct 4, immediately release the other hand to execute the same backward circular motion with the arm (Cts 5-7 [8]). The spine is now highly arched and the subsequent drop backward with the hips (Phrase 2) may be executed from this inverted hand position. However, when the backward arching is repeated, it is necessary to replace the hands in the original over-hold at the barre.

44. BACKWARD STRETCH

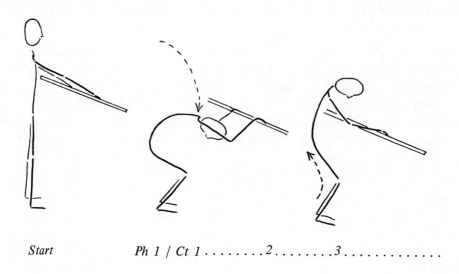

Start   *Ph 1 / Ct 1* . . . . *2* . . . .*3* . . . .

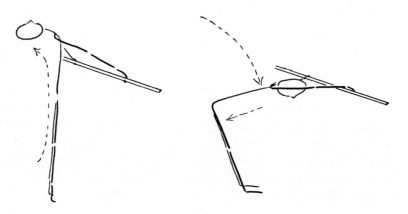

. . . . *4, 5, 6, 7 (or 8).*

Ph 2 / Use Cts 1 through 7 (or 8) to change from last position in previous phrase.

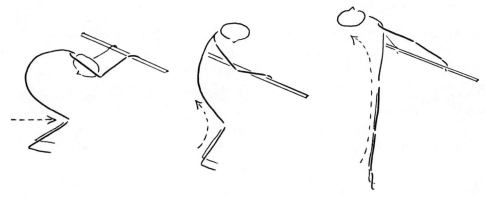

Ph 3 / Ct 1 . . . . *2* . . . . *3* . . . . *4, 5, 6, 7 (or 8)*.

Variation: Backward Stretch

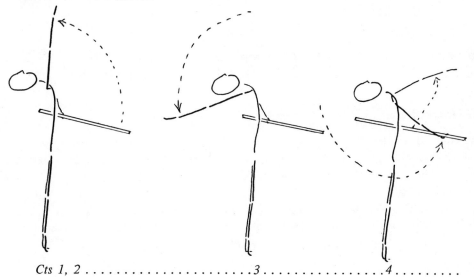

Cts 1, 2 . . . . *3* . . . . *4* . . . .

*Repeat same
with left*

*Hands cupped under
the barre for reverse
stretch.*

. . . *5, 6, 7 (or 8)*.

45. FORWARD STRETCH

Starting Position: Face the center of the room, feet together, hands holding the barre at nearly arm's length sideways and backward with a wide stretch from the shoulders. Body distance from barre is about 10″.

Phrase 1: (Cts 1-7 [8]). Bending the knees, drop the body over, head close to thighs, then start a forward succession, pulling up through the thighs, hips, torso, neck, and head while letting the hips fall toward the center of the room, hands remaining at the barre for support. The final position is a convex arch from the feet (on half-toe) to the top of the head, which has fallen backward.

Phrase 2: (Cts 1-7 [8]). A reverse curve for relaxation. Pulling the body backward into a concave position, bend the knees, drop the hips, and let the head fall close to the thighs, hands still holding the barre. This movement is almost identical with Phrase 1 of Exercise 43, except that the arms are holding the barre behind the body.

Repeat once or twice more.

Variation: A slow, sustained progression with leg extensions (forward) toward the center of the room, continuing from the above without interruption.

First Progression onto R foot

Bring the R knee forward and up to hip height as the body begins to open from the reverse curve (Cts 1-2); then extend the R leg forward, combining this stretch with an arching motion upward and backward from hips through head (Cts 3-4). The weight is now far forward causing the arms to let go of the barre. With the body still arching and keeping the hips well forward, step on the R foot, turning it out for sturdy support, and transfer the weight completely to the R foot (Cts 5-7 [8]). The arms are suspended about shoulder height behind the body.

Second Progression onto L foot

Continuing without stop, begin to draw the L leg forward from its rear position, coordinating with the arms which move in an under-curve, elbows leading, toward the front of the body and toward the center of the room. As the movement progresses, the torso drops forward and over the R leg which is bearing the body's weight (Cts 1-2). The L knee begins to lift forward (Cts 3-4). In moving rhythmically with the progression, the arms assist in stabilizing the body. They also lift in coordination with the lift of the L knee and, as the L leg is extended forward, they describe a forward circle, rising above the head at the same time as the full leg extension takes place. By the time the L foot is placed on the floor, the arms are opening far back of the head, the spine is arched, and the hips are well lifted (Cts 5-7 [8]).

Repeat both progressions at least twice if space permits.

Note: The Forward Stretch may be halted at any given point of the advance, provided that the weight is completely transferred to the advancing foot.

45. FORWARD STRETCH

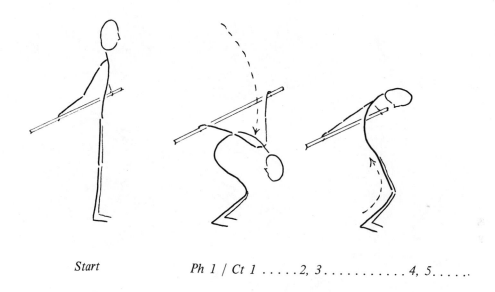

Start   *Ph 1 / Ct 1 . . . . .2, 3. . . . . .4, 5. . . . ..*

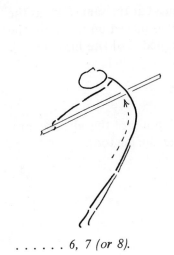

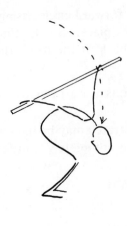

. . . . . . 6, 7 (or 8).

Ph 2 / Reverse curve. Use Cts 1 through 7 (or 8) to reach position shown.

Variation: First Progression onto Right Foot

Start   *Ct 1* . . . .*2* . . . .

. . . .*3* . . . .*4* . . . .*5, 6, 7 (or 8).*

Variation: Second Progression onto Left Foot

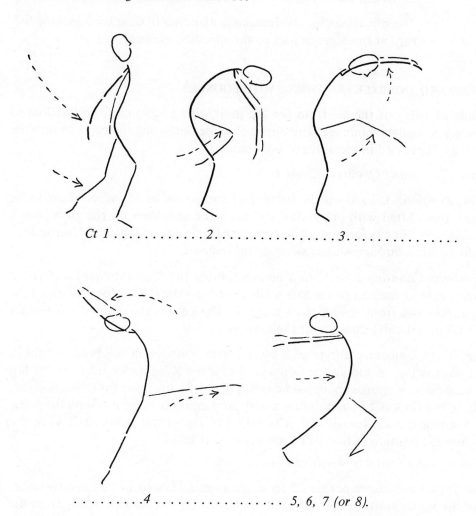

Ct 1 . . . . 2 . . . . 3 . . . .

. . . . 4 . . . . 5, 6, 7 (or 8).

SWINGS, BODY MOVEMENTS, LUNGES

The directions for the remaining exercises in Chapter 5 include the turn at the barre as part of the specified phrasing.

46. FORWARD AND BACK LEG SWINGS WITH BOUNCES

An isolated swing of the leg from the hip joint with a rebound from the floor to produce a secondary bounce. The entire exercise, including the turns to face the other way, is phrased in measures of 6/8 time.

Tempo: 76   *Music Quality:* Lively (6/8).

Starting Position: L hand on the barre, feet turned out at 45-degree angle, knees straight, torso lifted with pelvis directly under the shoulders (in the same plane), R arm at side. Focus forward. The body remains in this independent, unstrained upright position throughout the swinging movements.

Preparation: Counting 2 beats to a measure, bring the R arm forward on Cts 1-2 and then extend the arm to the side while stretching the R foot forward on Cts 3-4, leg turned out from the hip, toes pointed. The knee is straight and will remain straight (but not stiff) throughout the motion.

Phrase 1: An 8-measure phrase of 8 swings with bounces, in 6/8 time. Count in 6s for each swing, including the bounce. Swing the R leg backward from the hip with a turn-out of approximately 45 degrees (Cts 1-3), drop the foot, toes pointed, lightly to the floor (Ct 4) and rebound with suspension (Cts 5-6); reverse the direction, keeping the leg turned out (Cts 1-3), and repeat the bounce (Ct 4) in the same forward position as that of the preparation (Cts 5-6).

Repeat to make a total of 4 sets of swings.

Phrase 2: An 8-measure phrase of 16 single swings. Count in 3s for each swing. Swing the leg in positions described above backward and forward freely from the hip, finishing with the forward swing, which is held in the air.

Phrase 3: Suspension-Extensions. A total of 8 measures of 6/8 rhythm. Now count only 2 beats to the measure (on 1 and 4), and maintain the suspension-extension another 2 beats, making an accumulation of 4 Cts for each movement. Holding the R leg in the forward swing position (Cts 1-4), maintain the upright body position with shoulders down, torso lifted, hips even, and standing leg straight; R arm remains extended to the side. Carry the R leg sideways to suspend it, knee up (Cts 1-4). Then slowly lower the R leg, keeping it straight (Cts 1-4). Cross the R foot over the L, rise on half-toe turning toward the barre (Cts 1-2), to face the other direction, land in a turned-out position of both feet (Ct 3), and extend the outside (L) leg forward in preparation for a repeat of the movement (Ct 4). Arm likewise extends forward and to the side on Cts 3-4.

Repeat Phrase 1, 2, and 3 on the left, including turn.

46. FORWARD AND BACK LEG SWINGS WITH BOUNCES

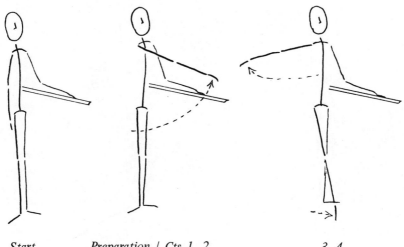

Start   *Preparation / Cts 1, 2 . . . . 3, 4.*

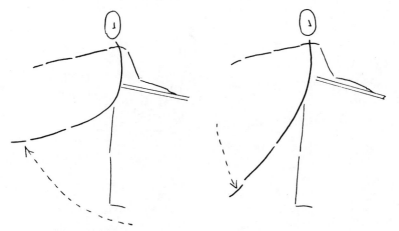

Ph 1 / Cts 1, 2, 3 . . . . 4. . . . .

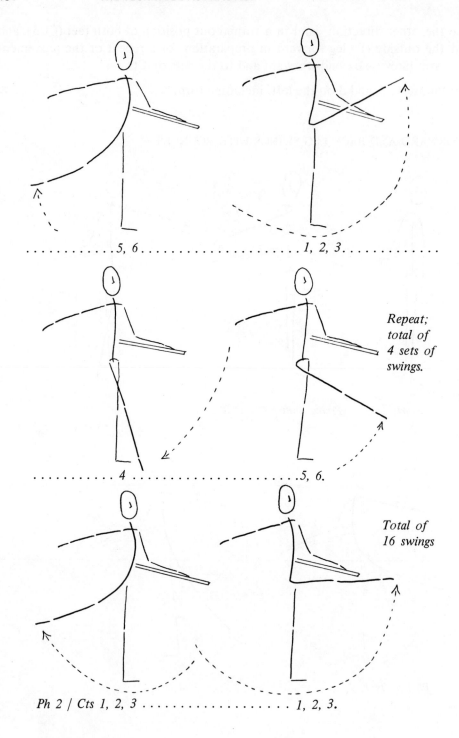

. . . . *5, 6* . . . . *1, 2, 3* . . . .

Repeat;
total of
4 sets of
swings.

. . . . *4* . . . . *5, 6.*

Total of
16 swings

Ph 2 / Cts 1, 2, 3 . . . . *1, 2, 3.*

Ph 3 / Hold: 1, 2, 3, 4 . . . . .1, 2, 3, 4 . . . .

. . . . .*1, 2, 3, 4* . . . .*1* . . . .*2* . . . .

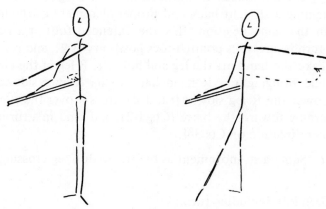

. . . . *3* . . . . *4.*

*Repeat on
left side.*

47. SIDEWAYS SWINGS WITH SUSPENSION-EXTENSIONS AND TURN

Tempo: 69   *Starting Position:* Same as above.

Preparation: Counting 2 beats to a measure, bring R arm forward on Cts 1-2 and extend the arm to the side while stretching the R foot across the L foot (Cts 3-4), well turned out with toes pointed. The hips remain facing front, as do the shoulders. Again, the working leg is stretched straight without rigidity.

Phrase 1: An 8-measure phrase of 8 swings with bounces, in 6/8 time. Count in 6s for each swing, including the bounce. Swing the R leg to the side (Cts 1-3), drop the foot lightly to the floor in a sideways, knee-turned-up position (Ct 4), and rebound with suspension (Cts 5-6). Without changing standing position, swing the R leg back across the body, knee turned up and slightly bent (Cts 1-3), drop the foot lightly to the floor in the same turned-out position as the preparation (Ct 4), and rebound lightly (Cts 5-6). Continue for a total of 8 swings with bounces.

Phrase 2: An 8-measure phrase of 8 single swings. The Tempo should be slower (66) than that of the Forward/Back Swings to allow for the greater strain the movements make on the body, sideways motion being less natural than forward/back motion.

Omitting the bounce, swing continuously from *in* to *out* with a freer motion in each direction. On the inward swing, the leg should be relaxed with the knee bending easily. The body remains independent of the leg motion and is erect without being stiff throughout the exercise.

Phrase 3: Suspension-Extension and Turn. A total of 12 measures. Count 2 beats to a measure. Swing the R leg sideways once more and catch it immediately with the R hand by gripping the calf muscle from the inside of the leg (Ct 1); hold the leg for Cts 2-4, maintaining a straight back and proper placement of the hips (under the shoulders). In the same position, flex the extended foot at a right angle to the leg (Ct 1), return to previous pointed-toes position (Ct 2), and repeat movements on Cts 3-4. Take the hand off the leg and hold the R leg in the air in its position (Cts 1-4) while bringing the R hand back to its former sideways shoulder-high position. Lower the R leg slowly (Cts 1-4), cross it over the standing leg, rise on half-toe turning toward the barre (Cts 1-2), and land in a turned-out position facing the other direction on Cts 3-4.

Preparation for the repeat: Same arm movement as before, with L leg crossing in front of R foot (Cts 1-4).

Repeat Phrases 1, 2, and 3 on left, including turn.

47. SIDEWAYS SWINGS WITH SUSPENSION-EXTENSIONS AND TURN

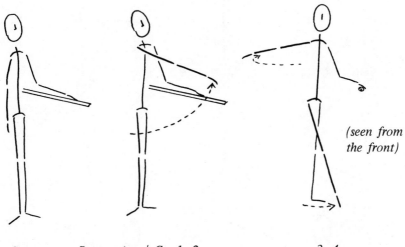

*(seen from
the front)*

Start   Preparation / Cts 1, 2 . . . . 3, 4.

Ph 1 / Cts 1, 2, 3 . . . . 4 . . . . 5, 6 . . . .

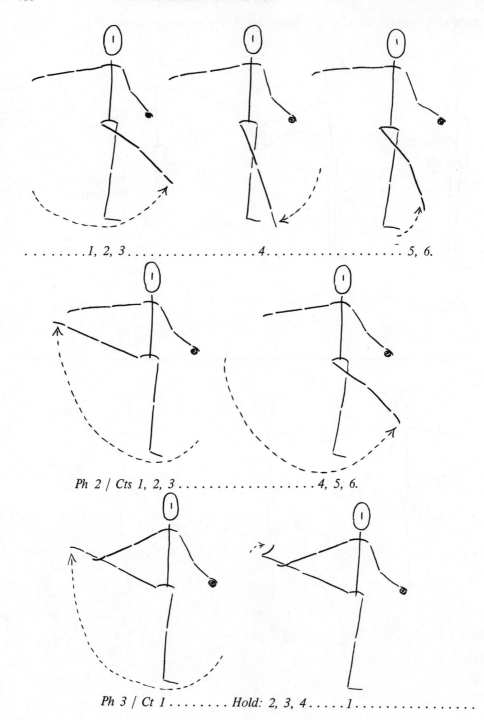

. . . .*1, 2, 3*. . . . . *4*. . . . . *5, 6.*

Ph 2 / Cts 1, 2, 3 . . . . *4, 5, 6.*

Ph 3 / Ct 1 . . . . *Hold: 2, 3, 4* . . . . . . *1*. . . . .

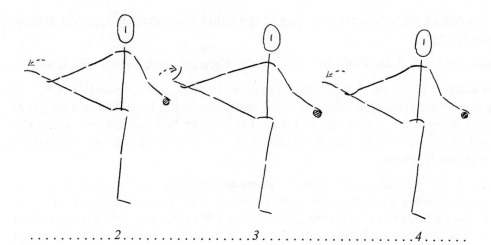

. . . . *2* . . . . *3* . . . . *4* . . . . . .

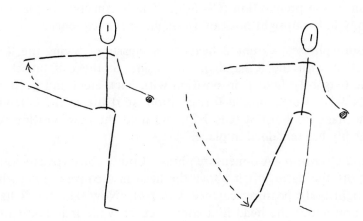

. . . . . . *1* . . . . *Hold: 2, 3, 4* . . . . . *1, 2, 3, 4.*

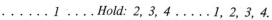

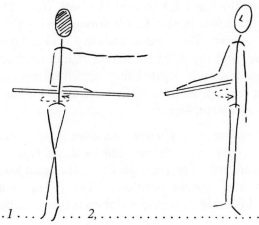

*Repeat preparation
and sequence on left.*

. . . . . . *1* . . . *J J* . . . *2,* . . . . *3, 4.*

48. CIRCULAR SWINGS WITH BOUNCES, SUSPENSION-EXTENSIONS, AND OVERDROP IN 6/8 RHYTHM

Tempo: 69   *Starting Position:* Same as for Forward/Back Swings with Bounces.

Preparation: Counting 2 beats to a measure, bring R arm forward on Cts 1-2, and then extend the arm outward while stretching the R leg to the side on Cts 3-4, foot turned out with pointed toes. The hips remain facing front, as do the shoulders. Raise the extended leg about 4" to 5" off the floor in preparation for a clockwise swing.

Phrase 1: An 8-measure phrase of 8 swings with bounces, in 6/8 time. Count in 6s for each swing, including the bounce. Swing the R leg in a circular motion inward, forward, upward, and outward, returning it to the point of departure (Cts 1-3). Touch the floor lightly with the toes (Ct 4), and rebound with suspension to the lifted position of the preparation (Cts 5-6). The R arm stays in place and the body is held firmly in the upright position throughout the sequence.

Phrase 2: A 4-measure phrase. Count 2 beats to a measure. Swing the R leg once more and catch it with the R hand on the inside, at the calf muscle, as it circles to the side (Cts 1-2), hold it in position with back erect and L (standing leg) straight (Cts 3-4). Remaining in this position, start lifting the extended leg higher, using the hand to hoist it (Cts 1-2), and hold the new position (Cts 3-4), making sure the hip has remained in place.

Phrase 3: Balance and Overdrop. A 8-measure phrase. Count 2 beats to a measure. Taking the L hand off the barre, lift it above the head in a convex curve while maintaining the upright body posture; balance (Cts 1-4). Now take the R hand off the leg, lift the arm above the head in a convex curve while maintaining the sideways suspension of the leg (Cts 1-4). Replace the L hand on the barre as the extended leg is turning out in the hip joint toward the back (Ct 1-2). While this movement is taking place, the torso begins to tilt forward with the R arm still framing the head in a convex curve. The motion ends in a forward overdrop with the R hand touching the floor and the R leg stretching high in the back (Cts 3-4). The total body design is now a sharply slanted line, the overdrop constituting a stretch of both the standing leg (L), which remains straight, and the steeply extended leg (R). Hold the overdrop for 4 beats.

Phrase 4: An Underswing Leading into a Turn. An 8-measure phrase including preparation for repeat (same counting). Swing the back leg from its high extended position down and forward (Cts 1-2); on Ct 2, the head and R arm rebound from the underswing into upright positions. The R leg then continues from front to side (Cts 3-4) in a sideways suspension-extension, as before. Hold the sideways extension (Cts 1-4). Lower the R leg, crossing it over the L foot (Cts 1-2), rise on half-toe and turn toward the barre with a high sideways pull through the torso to the left, R arm still overhead (Ct 3); land in the turned-out position facing the other direction (Ct 4).

Preparation for the repeat: Bring the L arm forward (Cts 1-2) and then to the side in an extended curve, while pointing the L foot to the side in a turned-out position (Cts 3-4). Raise the L foot in the air in preparation for the swing (Ct 4-"and").

Repeat the entire sequence with the L leg.

48. CIRCULAR SWINGS WITH BOUNCES, SUSPENSION-EXTENSIONS, AND OVERDROP IN 6/8 RHYTHM

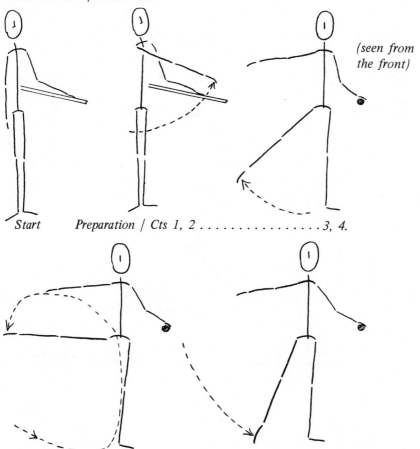

(seen from the front)

Start   Preparation / Cts 1, 2 . . . . 3, 4.

Ph 1 / Cts 1, 2, 3 . . . . 4 . . . .

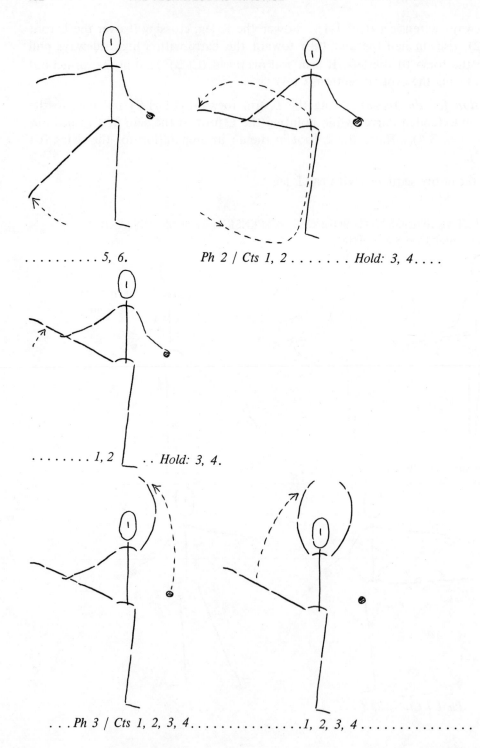

. . . . 5, 6.   Ph 2 / Cts 1, 2 . . . . Hold: 3, 4. . . .

. . . . 1, 2 . . Hold: 3, 4.

. . . Ph 3 / Cts 1, 2, 3, 4 . . . . 1, 2, 3, 4 . . . .

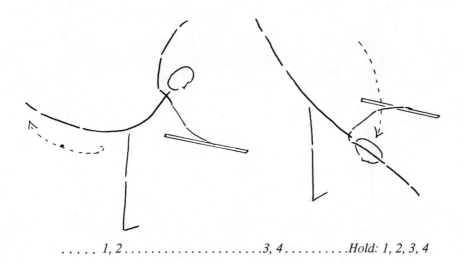

. . . . . 1, 2. . . . . .3, 4. . . . . .Hold: 1, 2, 3, 4

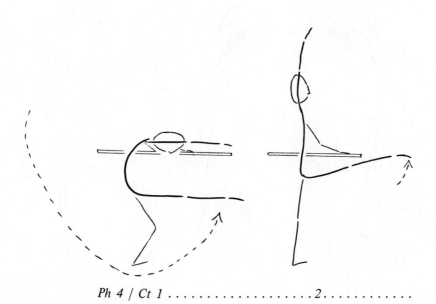

Ph 4 / Ct 1 .2. . . . .

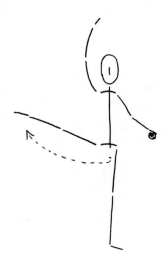

. . . . 3, 4 . . . . . . *Hold: 1, 2, 3, 4* . . . .

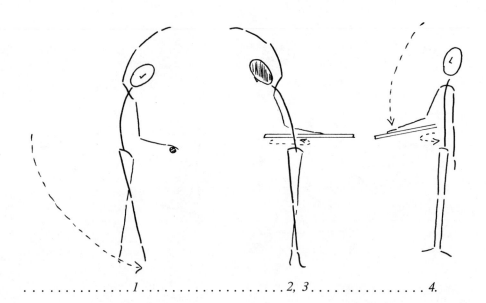

. . . . .1 . . . . .2, 3 . . . . 4.

*Repeat on
left.*

EXERCISE–STUDIES

49. BODY MOVEMENT WITH HALF-FALL

An Exercise-Study which explores a "double" rebound in terms of central body motion and ends with half-falls. Directions include sequences on both sides performed without interruption.

Count: Phrases of 8, with a preparation of 4 Counts. Practice without music first.

Tempo: 66   *Music Quality:* Resonant and sustained, 3/4 time suggested.

Starting Position: L hand on barre, elbow at ease, toes and heels together parallel to side wall, R arm at side. Body upright. Focus forward.

Preparation: Impulse in the knees initiates a modified sideways body succession on the right with the R arm softly lifting through the elbow, wrist, and hand (Cts 1-4). At the end of the succession (Ct 4), the head is looking up past the raised hand and the body is upright once more, but the heels have remained on the floor.

Phrase: Stretching the R arm backward from the high vertical position, as though describing the outline of a circle, bend the torso forward from the hips to make a flat horizontal line. Knees remain straight, and the R arm lines up alongside the body (Cts 1-4). Drop, bending the knees sharply and lifting the heels off the floor until they are nearly touching the buttocks; the R arm also falls but in doing so pulls forward through the elbow to make a convex curve (Ct 5). You are now rounded over, face close to knees, and the R arm is conforming to the curved body design. Rebound from this falling motion with an energetic thrust of the hips up under the torso, which remains rounded, though lifted to a higher plane (Ct 6). The arm is still convexly held, but it is higher as well. The upward tilted slant of the thighs is the same as in Excercise 30. The rebound movement continues upward as the knees begin to straighten (Ct 6-"and"), but before they are fully straight and while the back is still rounded over, a second "fall" occurs on Ct 7, in which the upper torso drops backward from the hips, and the R elbow bends sideways at shoulder height. Immediately, the R hand starts thrusting upward, palm pushing, as the body rebounds (Ct 7-"and"). In this recovery, both heels are lowered to the floor, and a vertical succession through the chest and head takes place (see Exercise 23, Variation with Vertical Arm Thrust), as the R hand stretches directly upward, head falling back, eyes focused on the hand (Ct 8).

Repeat 2 times to make a total of 3 times in all.

Turn: At the end of the repeats, keep the R arm overhead and extend the R leg sideways, foot turned out, toes pointed, in preparation for a sideways-pulling half-turn (Cts 1-2). Cross the R foot over the standing foot, rise on half-toe and slowly turn (Ct 3), R arm pulling overhead toward the wall; adjust the feet in parallel position as you face the other side (Ct 4).

Preparation for repeat: Other side. As R arm lowers to be placed on the barre, lift the L arm sideways in similar successional movements as previously described (Cts 5-8).

Repeat to make a total of 3 times on this side, turn as described (Cts 1-4), but on arrival adjust the feet and body to the following positions (Cts 5-8): parallel to each other and about 2″ apart, the L foot in advance of the R foot at a comfortable distance. (These directions should be adjusted according to leg and body proportions.) Outside arm pulls up slowly behind the body, both bending in convex curves. Feet rise to half-toe position. L hand on the barre.

Half-Fall and Recovery

Preparation: From this curved-over stance, bend the knees farther forward and drop over them into a crouching position (Ct 1) in preparation for a successional forward lift. The R arm swinging down, reverses its backward curve into a forward convex curve. By Ct 2, the lowest point of the drop has been reached and passed, and the body is beginning to rise successively with heels off the floor. The R arm coordinates with the rising movement by pulling up into a convex curve (Ct 3). By Ct 4, full height has been reached, knees are straight, the R arm overhead, and the eyes focused forward.

Half-Fall: Twist sharply through the shoulders and waist toward the center of the room, leaving the hips in place facing front (Ct 5); head and eyes also facing front. The R arm is curved above the head, framing it from the side and in the same plane as the shoulders. Still holding the barre, start bending the knees forward while pulling side-back with the torso. Keep the hips lifted, and descend with the R arm opening sideways and downward (Cts 6-7). By Ct 8, the hand has reached the floor, the torso remaining tilted to the side and backward; the thighs are still lifted; the R knee only is touching the floor. The hips are continuing to support most of the body's weight with the feet and toes assisting. The R elbow bends inward but does not touch the floor. Head is looking up, but it has not dropped back at the neck; it remains in line with the slant of the spine.

Recovery and Turn: A spiraling maneuver of the body negotiating the turn. Pull up from the Half-Fall position with an energetic overpull of the torso so that the weight is brought forward principally into the L foot (Ct 1). Describing a spiral half-turn toward the barre, keep lifting through the hips and body with the R arm curving forward successionally. Change hands at the barre, still curving over, as you swing around preparing to repeat the exercise on the other side (Ct 2). Placing the feet in the same relationship as before—inside foot forward, outside foot back (Cts 3-4)—draw the L arm upward and backward in a convex curves as you slowly rise to half-toes (Cts 5-8) with body lifting.

Repeat the Preparation and Half-Fall on the other side.

Variation: Full-Length Fall. Upon rising to the peak of the preparatory succession (Cts 1-4), take the inside hand off the barre. Both hands are now above the head in parallel position. Proceed with twist (see Half-Fall) on Ct 5, and descend side-back, letting both arms open to form a slanting line through the shoulders (Ct 6). As the R hand nears the floor (Ct 7), turn it sideways to catch the body's weight on the "karate" side of the palm while releasing R foot from a curled toe position to a relaxed foot (Ct 8). Slowly slide all the way to the floor until the body is prone on its side (Cts 9-12). The L arm has fallen to the left side of the body as this happens. Hold the fall (Cts 13-16).

49. BODY MOVEMENT WITH HALF-FALL

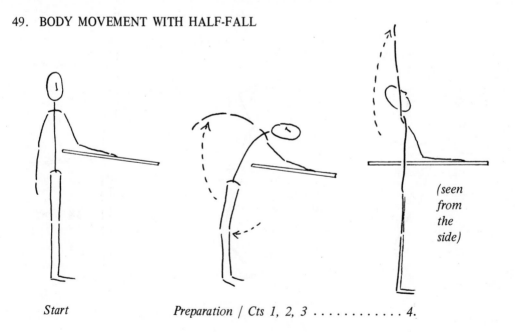

Start   *Preparation / Cts 1, 2, 3 . . . . 4.*

(seen
from
the
side)

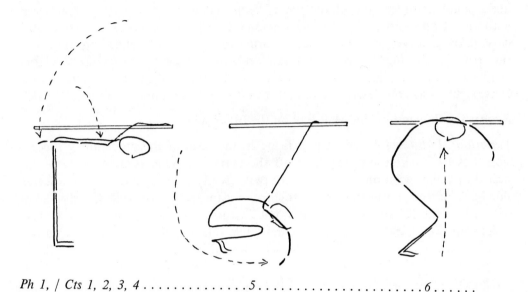

Ph 1, / Cts 1, 2, 3, 4 . . . . 5 . . . . 6 . . . . . .

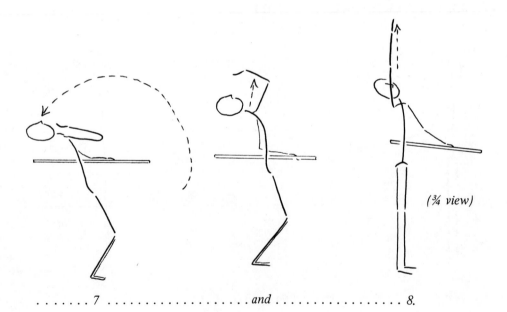

(¾ view)

. . . . 7 . . . . and . . . . 8.

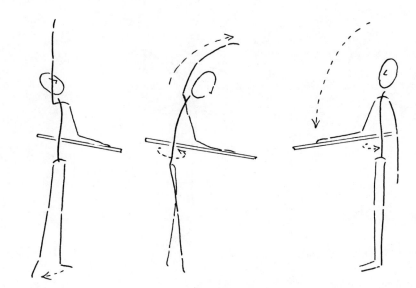

Turn / Cts 1, 2 . . . . *3* . . . . *4* . . . .

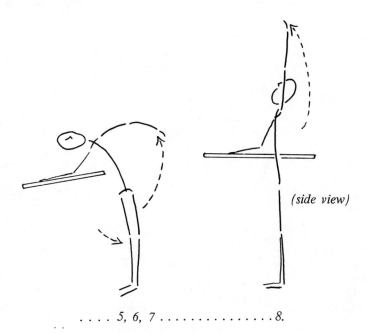

(side view)

. . . . *5, 6, 7* . . . . *8.*

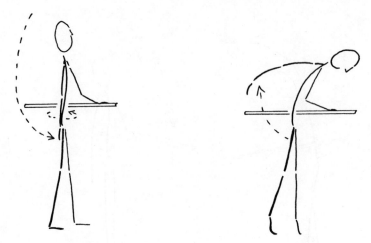

Final repeat / end turn on Ct 4, then .... 5, 6, 7, 8 ....

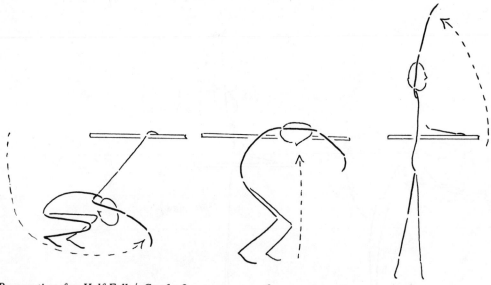

Preparation for Half-Fall / Cts 1, 2..........3..................4......

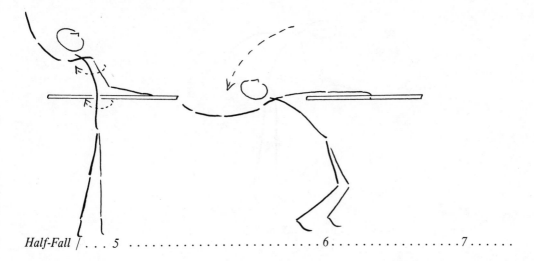

Half-Fall / . . . 5 . . . . 6 . . . . 7 . . . . . .

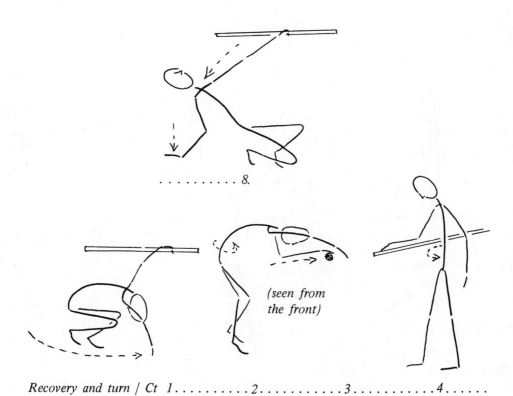

. . . . 8.

*(seen from
the front)*

Recovery and turn / Ct 1 . . . . 2 . . . . 3 . . . . 4 . . . . . .

. . . . 5, 6, 7, 8 .

Variation: Full-length Fall

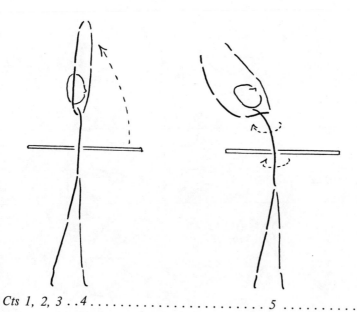

Cts 1, 2, 3 . . 4 . . . . 5 . . . .

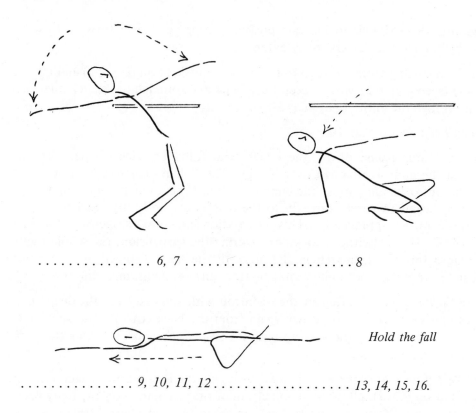

. . . . *6, 7* *8*

Hold the fall

. . . . *9, 10, 11, 12* . . . . *13, 14, 15, 16.*

50. SWINGS WITH CIRCULAR SUCCESSIONS

Demanding considerable strength in the thighs and back, as well as steady balance, Swings with Circular Successions are the hallmark of early Humphrey Technique. The barre provides a necessary support when practicing the movement, which cannot be executed alone until the dancer has attained a thorough understanding of, and ability to perform, complete body successions. Two pendulum-like swings, from front to back and reverse, serve as preparation for the circular succession, making three movements in all.

Count: In 8s to make 1 phrase. Four phrases to complete the exercise, including the turn to face the other side. A preparation of 4 Counts.

Tempo: 63 *Music Quality:* Surging, resonant.

Starting Position: L hand on barre, feet parallel, about 2″ apart, with L foot in advance of R foot at an easy distance. This position should be secure and comfortable. (Adjust placement according to leg and body proportions.)

Preparation: Rise slowly to half-toe position, bringing R arm forward to waist height, palm facing in, fingers softly extended.

Phrase 1: Swinging from front to back with the outside arm (Cts 1-2) and reverse (Cts 3-4) in conjunction with a deep knee bend and rounded back; a circular succession through the entire body (Cts 5-8).

Front to Back Swing. Cts 1-2.

As the R arm swings down, the knees bend fully, bringing the heels off the floor, and the body is rounded over (Ct 1). The R hand has passed close to the floor, the buttocks are almost touching the lifted heels. On the upswing (Ct 2), the R arm begins to curve convexly to the rear as the body lifts, and the movement is slowing up appreciably. This deceleration leads into a suspension, in which the knees straighten (without locking). During the suspension, the whole figure is making a forward semi-arch in the air with the head dropped over from the neck, and a strong upward pull is coursing through the thighs, hips, and torso.

Reverse Swing. Cts 3-4. Repeat the overdrop with the body and the deep knee-bend as you swing the R arm down again from the back (Ct 3). Rise once more to half-toe as you swing the arm up with the suspension approximating the starting position (Ct 4).

Phrase 2: Circular Succession. Cts 5-8. Swinging the R arm down again with the body overdrop (Ct 5), allow the momentum of the swing to carry the body backward instead of lifting it upward, thus opening the torso and lifting the hips immediately after the lowest point of the swing (Ct 6). This position serves as the beginning of the successional movement which pulls progressively through hips, torso, arm, and head. As the body unfolds, and the hips lift, the chest drops back with the head and shoulders dropping as well. The arm has swung low, well behind the body. The effort to rise is now clearly seen. The movement is slowing up, and there is an obvious sense of weightedness in the action of successively lifting the torso and head (Ct 7). By Ct 8, the body has attained the highest point of suspension; the arm is stretching upward over the head, the legs are pulled straight (without locking), and another forward drop is imminent. The motion which follows begins the repeat of the entire phrase (Cts 1-8).

Repetition: A total of 3 phrases, followed by a slow half-turn (to face the other side), similar to the half-turn described in the preceding exercise (49). With the conclusion of the turn, which lasts 4 Cts, place the R hand on the barre, the R foot in advance of the L foot (as before), and rise on half-toe with the outside (L) arm pulling forward as before (Cts 5-8).

Repeat for a total of 4 phrases, including the turn.

Exercise 49 Swings with Circular Successions (Phrase 1, Count 6): Mira Pospisil

Note: Coordination of breath is of importance in helping maintain balance and movement flow.

Variation: Leg Extension and Backward Turn. Cts 1-8. Repeat 3 phrases of the Swings with Circular Successions but, as the final succession is being completed, draw the outside leg (R) forward when the R arm reaches the crest of the circle (Ct 8 of the preceding phrase). On Ct 1, swing the R leg forward and simultaneously drop the R arm and upper torso forward. The leg has shot up to hip height and the arm is almost touching it. The body design is elliptical with the weight on the L leg. On Ct 2, carry the extended leg, knee turned up and straight, to the outside in a wide curve; at the same time, lift the body and the arm upward to near straightness (arm frames the head); continuing, carry the extended leg (turned out from the hip joint) toward the back (Ct 3), and, lowering it, place the foot on half-toe in parallel positioning to the rear of the standing foot, which by now has risen to half-toe. On Ct 4, the R arm drops to its side, and the body begins to fall side-back as though into a half-fall, but the movement is not completed, for a "rebound" takes place on Ct 5, consisting of an additional lift and an additional side-back pull through the torso culminating in an outside backward half-turn (Ct 6). This turn, executed slowly on half-toe, forces the L arm to leave the barre as the torso pulls more and more to the right. With the body now facing the other side (Ct 7), the L arm swings down and forward to resume the starting position facing the other direction (Ct 8).

Repeat the 3 phrases of the Swings with Circular Successions, the Leg Extension, omit the Backward Turn, and terminate instead with a Half-Fall, taking the inside (R) arm off the barre and holding it above the shoulder in a straight line as the body drops side-back (Cts 5-8). The Half-Fall is the same as in Exercise 49.

50. SWINGS WITH CIRCULAR SUCCESSIONS

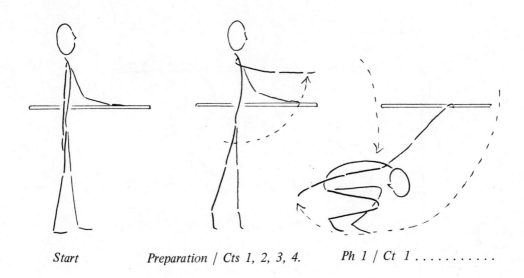

Start   *Preparation | Cts 1, 2, 3, 4.*   *Ph 1 | Ct 1 . . . .*

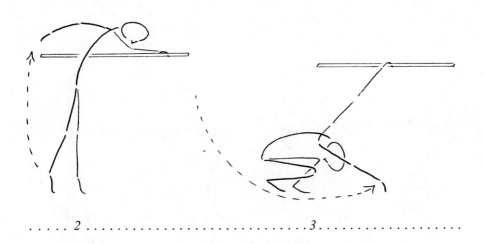

. . . . . . 2 . . . . 3 . . . .

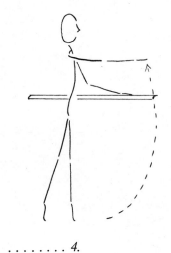

. . . . 4.

Ph 2 / Ct 5 . . . .

. . . . .6. . . . . .7. . . . . .8.

Variation: Leg Extension and Backward Turn

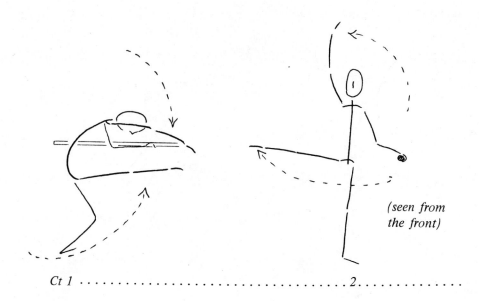

Ct 1 . . . . *2*. . . . .

*(seen from
the front)*

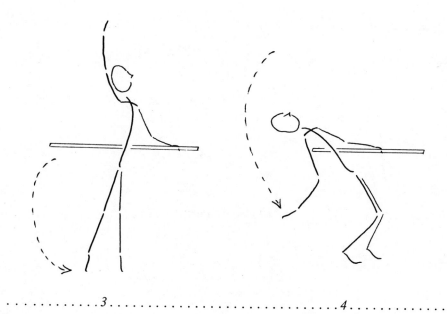

. . . .*3*. . . . .*4*. . . . .

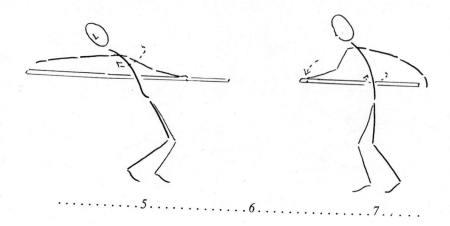

. . . . 5 . . . . 6 . . . . 7 . . . . .

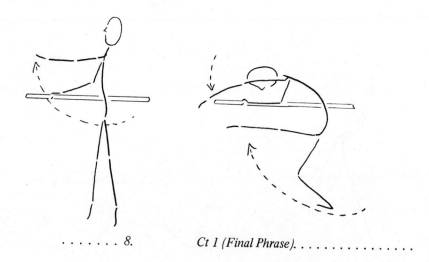

. . . . 8.   *Ct 1 (Final Phrase).* . . . .

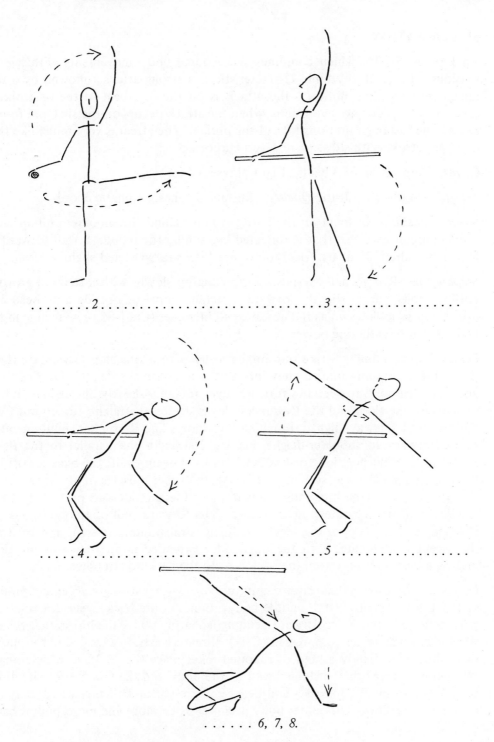

.... 2 .... 3 ....

...... 4 .... 5 ....

...... 6, 7, 8.

51. LUNGE STUDY

An Exercise-Study, which combines successional body movements with leg extensions. Its chief rhythmic characteristic is a strong attack followed by a sustained reverberating motion: the attack is on the first beat of the 6-Ct phrase (except in the sideways extensions, when the attack occurs on the first and fourth beats); the sustained motions fill out the phrase. The effect is very much like that of a gong stroke with subsequent reverberations.

Count: Preparation of 3 beats. Eight phrases of 6s.

Tempo: 44 (Slow)   *Music Quality:* Sustained tones, emphatic chords.

Starting Position: L hand on the barre, R arm behind the shoulder pulling backward in a convex curve that is reflected in a similar torso pull. L foot forward of R, parallel, about 2″ apart. Heels on floor. Focus forward and slightly down.

Preparation: Rise to half-toe position, pulling up slowly with a sense of growing tension; body curves slightly forward matching curve of outside arm; head and eyes begin to look down as the upward pull increases (Cts 1-3). The feeling in the body is that of gathering power.

Phrase 1: The Lunge. Strike out emphatically with a long step forward on the L (inside) leg, dropping immediately into a deep lunge on that leg (Ct 1). The torso does not cave in, but stretches forward; eyes focused directly ahead. The L heel remains on the floor and the R (outside) leg is stretched straight, turned out from the hip, foot sideways lightly touching the floor. The R arm has simultaneously swung forward to shoulder-height, making a straight line parallel to the floor. Eyes front. Hold position for Cts 2-3. On Ct 4 begin to lift the back leg off the floor, keeping the knee straight and using the thigh muscles of the forward leg for body support (the hips must remain under the shoulders as part of the torso and *not* pull up separately in the rear). The forward pull of the body has not changed, but the supporting leg is gradually straightening (Ct 5), and by Ct 6 the ascent is complete, with the outside leg extended in an arabesque position, making a long, taut line from the back foot to the forward stretched hand.

Phrase 2: Oppositional Successional-Extension. With a strongly accented impulse in the L knee, contract the middle body, rounding the back, head down; at the same time, pull the R leg forward bending it sharply under the hip so that the entire torso seems to be compressed (Ct 1). Breath has been expelled in this movement, but immediately a kind of rebound takes place (Cts 2-3), in which inhalation coordinates with a sustained pull of the body and the legs in opposite directions. The feeling is that of a coil being compressed and then released, only the release is very slow. The center body begins to open more and more, pulling backward with tension as the R arm is drawing back over the face and head in a progressive bend through the elbow, wrist, and hand, at the same time, the R leg, pulling through the knee (which is now facing up) is beginning to extend forward into a straight line (Cts 4-5). By Ct 6, the suspension-extension is complete, and the line of the body is horizontal from the extended foot to the extended hand with the supporting leg slightly bent. In achieving this fully stretched position, the breath is slowly exhaled.

Phrase 3: Sideways Successional-Extension. Again, a sudden coiling movement of contracting the torso (this time with an intake of breath), bringing the R knee inward under the body as well as inward toward the barre. The L knee bends as well. The R arm simultaneously pulls downward from the back to the side, and then sharply inward with elbow leading, forearm lying sideways, and palm twisted to face up (Ct 1). This spasmodic accented compression of the body, head, and arm is followed immediately by an uncoiling motion begun quickly and ending slowly (Cts 2-3): the R knee pulls up in front of the chest, while the R arm pulls upward in a convex curve over the head, both of these movements triggering the parallel sideways extensions of the arm and leg. These uncoiling extensions are executed successionally outward through the leg and arm while the standing leg (L) is straightening. (The weight has remained on the L leg, heel down, throughout the above movements.) Once again, the effect is that of a sustained reverberation through the whole body. A quick repeat of the inward coiling motion and another suspension-extension of the outside arm and leg to the side on Cts 4-6.

Phrase 4: Half-Fall and Turn. From the culminating point of the second sideways successional-extension, bring the R leg circularly back to place the foot on half-toe on the floor in preparation for a half-fall. In executing this motion, there is a strong lift in the torso and the R arm rises into a high curved position as the shoulders twist sideways (Ct 1). The Half-Fall, etc., being similar to, but not identical with, the Half-Fall, etc., of Exercise 49, descriptions will be given in detail. Shoulders and hips twist into a frieze-like position to face the center of the room while knees remain pointing forward (Ct 1). Descend into a half-fall, bringing the R hand to the floor, and look upward, holding the neck and head in a line with the slanting torso (Cts 2-3). The speed of the fall gradually accelerates so that a rebound on Ct 4 automatically pulls the body up. With a sideways swing-lift of the R arm, drop forward, cross the R foot over the L foot, and negotiate the turn in a spiraling form. The speed of the recovery decelerates as the body pulls up slowly (Ct 5) facing the opposite direction. It is now in position with the R foot in advance of the L foot, the L arm pulling back of the shoulder into a convex curve, to repeat the movement on the other side.

Phrases 5, 6, and 7: Repetition of Phrases 1, 2, and 3 with other leg.

Phrase *8: Final Fall.* Twisting to the side in preparation for the fall, raise both arms over the head in parallel position (Ct 1). Descend slowly on a slant from fingertips to knees (Cts 2-3). By Ct 4, the L knee is on the floor as well as the L hand, and the body is sharply angled to the side-back. Sliding on the "karate" side of the hand, the dancer smoothly descends full length to the floor, while the R arm slowly pressing sideways-down lines up alongside the body, resting lightly on the R hip (Cts 5-6). A retard in the musical accompaniment is suggested to bring the Study to completion.

51. LUNGE STUDY

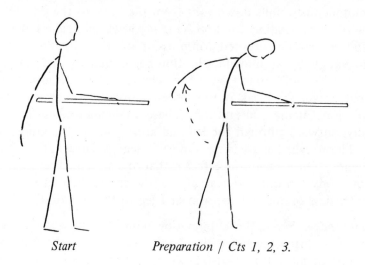

Start   *Preparation | Cts 1, 2, 3.*

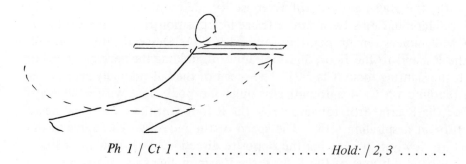

Ph 1 | Ct 1 . . . . Hold: | 2, 3 . . . . . .

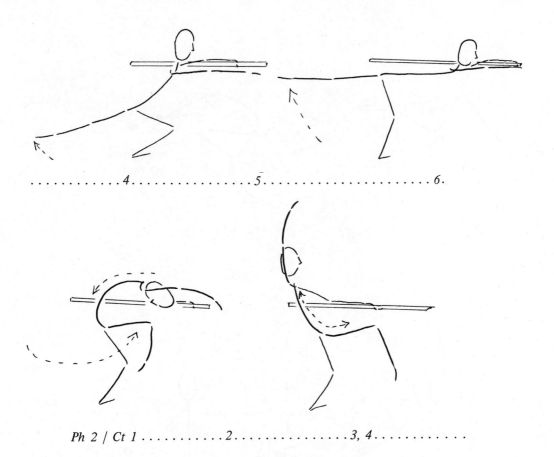

. . . . *4* . . . . *5* . . . . *6.*

Ph 2 / Ct 1 . . . . *2* . . . . *3, 4* . . . .

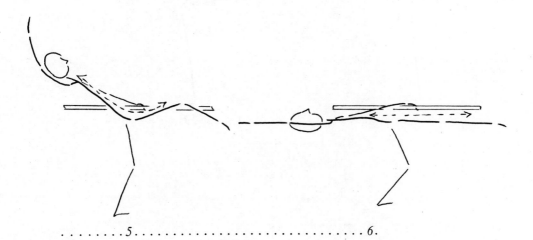

. . . . *5* . . . . *6.*

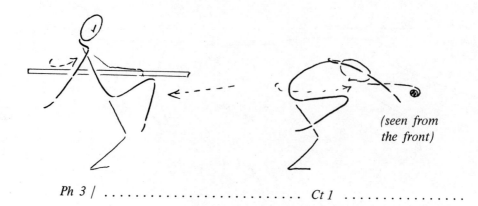

Ph 3 / . . . . Ct 1 . . . .

(seen from the front)

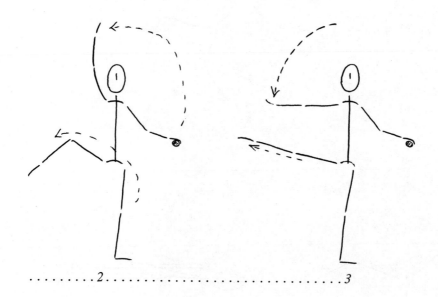

. . . . 2 3

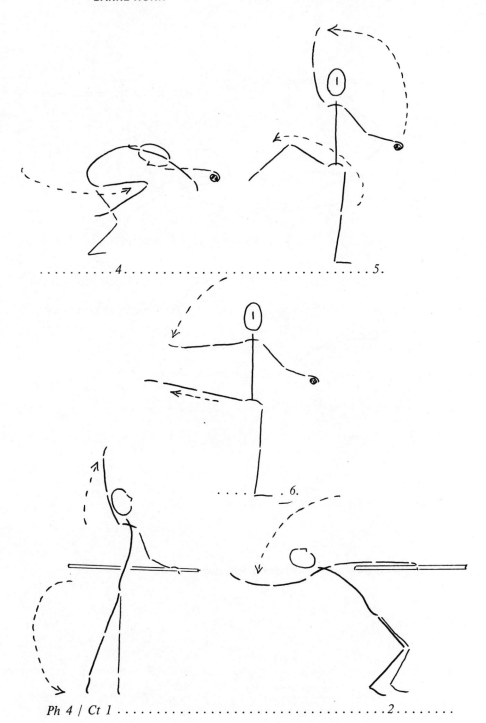

4. . . . . 5.

. . . . . . 6.

Ph 4 / Ct 1 . . . . 2 . . . .

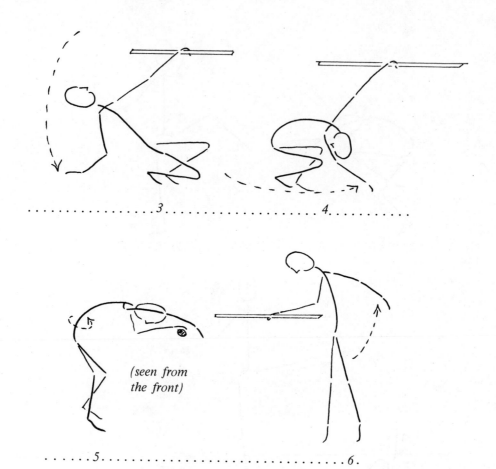

(seen from the front)

Repeat first three phrases on left side

Ph 5 . . . . . Ph 6 . . . . Ph 7.

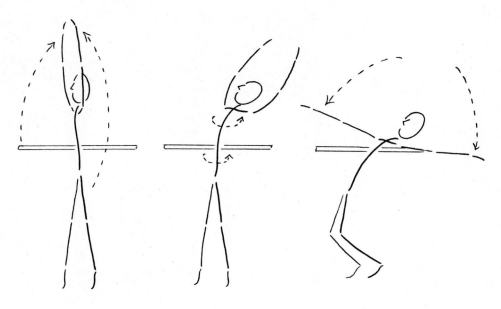

Ph 8 / Ct 1 . . . . *2* . . . . *3* . . . .

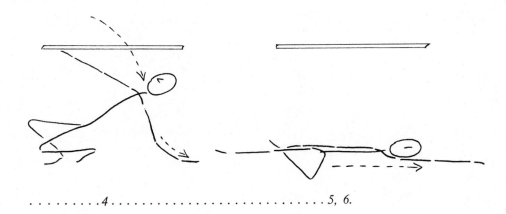

. . . . *4* . . . . *5, 6.*

Chapter 6
SPATIAL SEQUENCES

INTRODUCTION

Doris Humphrey's choreography was never more striking than when she expressed her "love of rhythm" in movements which swept across the stage, gathering momentum in shimmering leaps and turns, changing direction playfully, or building pattern after pattern of grand architectural design. The paths she charted through space pulsated with complex rhythms, sometimes in counterpoint to the music. When there was no music, the movement phrases punctuated time as well as space. In Doris Humphrey's dances, rhythm was the animating force—proof of the life that existed in the "arc between two deaths."

Rhythmic training is, therefore, of utmost importance in learning the Humphrey style. When shifting from the more or less restricted positions involved in Center, Floor, and Barre Work to movement through space, the need to clarify rhythmic emphasis increases. For this reason, we have started the section on Spatial Sequences with a series of elementary rhythms based on natural "locomotive" movements such as running and leaping.

In these fundamental motions of the human body lies the secret of rhythmic coordination: oppositional flow, which ensures balance, is produced involuntarily. In general, the dancer elaborates upon coordinations which are inborn. Another elementary rhythmic coordination is established with the Slide-Leaps sequence. Here, the arms, swinging in parallel motion, join the legs only on the leap. Once the innate feeling of rhythmic phrasing is established consciously as dance movement, the student should be able to handle more difficult assignments: triplets (slow and fast, combined with arm movements, turns, and so on) and extended dance motions in a variety of counts.

Toward the end of a lesson with Doris Humphrey, it was customary to be given the challenging and rewarding opportunity of learning excerpts from her compositions. Inspired by this procedure, and wishing to keep the suggested lesson format in this book close to that of remembered classes, I have chosen to conclude Part Two with a presentation of movement phrases from *Water Study, The Shakers,* and *Passacaglia.* While it is difficult to translate into words the rhythmic-dynamic content—let alone the spirit—of the unique movements Doris Humphrey created for the stage, these excerpts are presented to provide the exciting experience of studying whole dance phrases composed by a master craftsman in the art of choreography.

52. RUNNING AND LEAPING PATTERNS IN 4/4 RHYTHMS

For rhythmic training. Starting with two measures of each rhythm, then only one measure, the exercise aims to develop speed and fluency in natural coordinations. Arms swing oppositionally on every quarter-note beat, are held on eighth-note beats. Use quarter-notes for leaps, eighth-notes for runs.

Please note: The forward running/leaping leg has a natural bend of the knee, not the straightened knee position associated with balletic leaps. The back leg is stretched as much as possible in flight. The body, as described in Running and Leaping as Dance Experience, pp. 26-27, is angled forward.

Tempo: Allegro   *Music Quality:* Strongly accented. Drum beat is also effective and can be used, when efficiency is gained, as counterpoint.

Movement Path: From stage left, clockwise in a circle; from stage right, counterclockwise in a circle.

Starting Position: For clockwise path, from the far left upstage corner, face the periphery of an imaginary circle. Weight on R foot, L foot pointed forward in readiness for a step on Ct 1. R arm stretched forward in unstrained opposition to L leg, L arm is swung oppositionally to the rear.

Accompaniment should provide a two-measure introductory phrase. Two measures for each rhythm. When mastered, one measure for each rhythm, and a repeat of the final rhythm (Variation VI) to conclude the exercise effectively.

1st Rhythm: Straight leaping on quarter-note beats: 1-2-3-4
2nd Rhythm: Double-time running: 1-"and"-2-"and"-3-"and"-4-"and"
3rd Rhythm: Variation I: 1-2-3-"and"-4
4th Rhythm: Variation II: 1-"and"-2-3-4
5th Rhythm: Variation III: 1-2-"and"-3-4
6th Rhythm: Variation IV: 1-2-3-4-"and"
7th Rhythm: Variation V: 1-"and"-2-3-"and"-4
8th Rhythm: Variation VI: 1-"and"-2-"and"- 4

Note: On the 2nd Rhythm (double time), the arms are not swung at all, but held firmly alongside the body. In the final variation (VI), the arms are lifted to shoulder height, R arm leading when running clockwise (L arm, when running counter-clockwise) with the body turned somewhat sideways, facing out; on Ct 3 of the run, swing the back arm in a forward circle simultaneously with the leap, still holding the advancing arm in place. Then resume the running with both arms extended as before.

Repeat in counter-clockwise motion, starting with the R foot from the upstage-right corner of the room.

Variation: Change the order of the rhythms, and combine the running/leaping sequences with sudden changes to walking sequences, in which the legs accentuate the double-time beats by stepping down more emphatically or more lightly.

53. SLIDING AND LEAPING PATTERNS IN 6/8 RHYTHMS

For preliminary training in aerial motion. The movement consists of a slide followed immediately by a hop. As the hop progresses forward as well as upward, the movement is called a "slide-leap" rather than a "slide-hop" because it evokes a sense of flight.

Movement Path: Clockwise in a circle or a diagonal cross from upstage left or right to the opposite corner.

Tempo: (6/8 time) Allegro Vivace   *Music Quality:* Sparkling.

Starting Position: Facing direction of Movement Path, R foot pointed forward, arms extended at shoulder height, torso and face lifted expectantly.

Phrase: Two measures, allowing for 2 sets of slide-leaps, starting with the R foot. Counting in 6s, slide forward with the R foot leading (Cts 1-3), stepping on the R again for the hopping motion (Cts 4-5), land on the R on Ct 6. In performing the hop on the forward (R) leg, the back leg is lifted off the floor from the hip; the L knee is stretched backward without stiffness and the toes are pointed. The torso lifts in the hopping action and the head is turned easily toward the L shoulder as though looking over the shoulder at the back leg. Repeat with the L leg taking the slide and the leap, head looking over R shoulder on the leap.

Arm Patterns

A rhythmic coordination of both arms swinging together from one side to the other on the 4th beat of every measure.

Starting Position: Facing direction of Movement Path, both arms lifted to the left side as the body bends at the waist to the right; R foot pointed forward.

Phrase: Cts 1-6, repeated. Slide-leap as above, but swing the arms from left to right on the count of 4, while springing onto the R foot for the hop. The arms assist the body in taking off from the floor. The bend in the waist is strongly accented with this movement, and the head looks over the L shoulder as before.

Repeat with the L leg taking the slide and the leap and the arms swinging from right to left on the 4th beat.

Note: On Cts 1, 2, and 3, the arms are held in the position of the previous swing. Repeat counter-clockwise with the L foot starting the slide and the leap, and the arms swinging first from right to left.

Suggested Variation: 2 Triplets followed by 1 Slide-Leap, making an alternate pattern over 2 phrases. Arms alongside the body on Triplets, lift to open side positions for Slide-Leap.

Variation: With Turns. Principally a sideways motion, the Slide-Leaps with Turns progress forward as well, but in turning, the slide is transformed into a jump. Both arms are loosely wrapped around the body (R arm in front, L arm in back) on the turn (Cts 1-3), then are swung out to the same side, as before, on the leaps (Cts 4-6).

Tempo and *Music Quality:* Same as above.

Starting Position: Facing front, upstage center, arms at sides, R foot pointed diagonally forward to the right.

Phrase: On Ct 1, step lightly on the right foot bending the knee forcibly and immediately take off into a jump-turn (Ct 2), landing on the L foot (Ct 3), facing front. Swinging the arms and the body to the right, spring onto the R foot (Cts 4-5), landing on the R foot on Ct 6. The L foot is extended freely sideways-left during this hopping motion, and is ready to slide to the left for a repeat of the slide-leap without a turn, arms swinging now to the left. Progress in this zigzagging motion down through the room.

Repeat with the jump-turn, etc., to the left and the slide-leap to the right without a turn.

54. TRIPLETS WITH FALLING MOTIFS

Movement in 3/4 time demanding contrapuntal body rhythms of an involved nature. If, in music, counterpoint is basically "the art of combining melodies"[1] then counterpoint in dance is the art of combining diverse rhythms through coordinated motion. In Triplets with Falling Motifs, the task is to maintain a quick 3-beat pattern with the feet while executing arm and body movements in a slow 4/4 time. The addition of the fall/recovery motif introduces dynamics of a pronounced kind which create an additional factor: phrasing, which has a life of its own, so to speak, within a given duration of so many measures (in this case, 4 measures). The following directions make an attempt to break down the total action into component parts so that one rhythm can be practiced alone before being combined and synchronized with the secondary rhythm.

Preliminary Practice for Triplets

First, a series of triplets to be performed continuously for rhythmic accuracy and physical dexterity. Speed increases from slow to fast.

Tempo: (3/4 time) Andante accelerating to Allegro *Music Quality:* From smoothly flowing with mild emphasis on the first triplet beat to vigorous and brisk with strong emphasis on the first triplet beat.

Movement Path: Clockwise and counter-clockwise.

Starting Position: For clockwise path, body held erect without stiffness, facing periphery of circle, R foot pointed forward to take initial step. Arms held easily alongside body.

---

[1] Counterpoint, *Encyclopaedia Britannica* (Chicago, William Benton, Publisher, 1962) Vol. 6, p. 594.

Triplet

Stepping R-L-R (down-up-up) with weight falling on the first step, knee bent as entire foot is placed on the floor, 2nd and 3rd steps on half-toe, knees straight. The next triplet starts with the L foot leading. Throughout the movement the torso remains lifted, the shoulders down, arms at sides. Avoid shifting shoulders and swinging hips as the tempo increases.

Repeat (for practice) in counter-clockwise direction starting with the L foot.

Preliminary Practice for Arms and Body

Count in slow 4s. Standing in place (feet together), arms at sides. Cross arms in front of body (Ct 1), lift them up successively in front of the face and above the head (Ct 2); open them outward to shoulder height (Ct 3), and lower them to Starting Position (Ct 4).

Triplets Combined with Arm and Body Movements

Movement Path: Clockwise and counter-clockwise.

Starting Position: Same as above for Triplet Practice. Arms now move contrapuntally in the slow 4/4 rhythm against the quick 3/4 rhythm of the feet. Practice for smooth articulation and synchronization.

Arm and Body Preliminary Practice for Falling Motions

Starting Position: Arms lifted above the face, palms turned out. Body is lifted as well, facing front. Legs wide apart, feet turned out at a 45-degree angle. The arm movement is similar in quality to the drop and rebound of Exercise 18.

Without music, first let the L arm drop sideways with the body and head falling sideways with it. Contrary to Exercise 18, do not rebound by retracing the falling pattern but continue the swing circularly inward, bringing the arm across the body and upward to its starting position. In doing so, the acceleration and deceleration of weight is clearly felt in the phrasing of both the arm and torso. Now practice the same movement on the right, letting the R arm take the torso and head with it as it falls and recovers in a circular pattern. The eyes look up as the drop occurs and then focus forward with the return to the initial position.

Triplets Combined with Falling Motion

Movement Path: Clockwise and counter-clockwise.

Starting Position: For clockwise path, body faces the periphery of the circle from an upstage point. R foot pointed forward to take initial step. Torso lifted, arms overhead, palms facing out. Focus high.

Maintaining the triplet, add the arm movements on the following counts: Holding the arms in the overhead position for 2 beats (2 triplets), start the falling motion to the L side on Ct 3, pass through the deepest point of the descent with increasing speed of body motion and recover as the 4th measure is in effect, slowing up toward the highest point of the circle.

Repeat the pattern as an entire sequence.

Note: On all clockwise movements, the Falling Motion is performed on the left. For counter-clockwise movements, the Falling Motion is on the right with the R arm circling down.

55. TURNS

While Humphrey turns are considerably varied in the way the body, head, and arms coordinate with the legs and feet, the turn that is most frequently seen in the choreographer's pure dance motifs is a form of spiraling, which uses successional movement in relation to gravitational pull. As the body revolves around its own axis, the effect is that of fluent suspension. (The "axis", of course, is an imaginary line conceived to be centered in the torso, analogous to the earth's imaginary axis.) In the successional or spiral turn, as in the Circular (Spiral) Fall (Exercise 41), speed is variable, dependent on weight placement during the action. The movements of the arms and the free leg are also variable. There are innumerable Humphrey turning motions involving the body in unorthodox configurations.[1]

It is necessary, however, to limit our descriptions to two kinds of basic turns: "outside" and "inside",[2] and those executed while performing triplets.

Outside Turns: a term used to describe a turn which revolves in the same direction as the leg on which the body pivots, i.e., to the right on the R leg.

Inside Turns: a term used to describe a turn in the opposite direction from the leg on which the body pivots, i.e., to the right on the L leg.

---

[1]One such memorable example was Doris Humphrey's early solo, *Gigue* (Bach), in which she performed a continuous hopping turn on one leg while executing fluent arm and body motions.

[2]These turns, as designated, are the opposite of ballet turn terminology: "en dehors" and "en dedans".

Outside Turns, Suggested Practice

Count: 6 (2 Triplets), involving 5 steps, traveling.

Tempo: Andante to Allegro according to balancing and spinning needs.

Stepping forward L-R-L (Cts 1-2-3), transfer the weight from the L foot on Ct 3 to the R foot (Ct 4) with an impulse in the L knee and a quick step up on half-toe by the R foot. The R knee is flexed as the weight is transferred. (In practice the extended leg [L] is lifted freely off the ground and suspended with knee slightly flexed and turned out behind the body as the spin takes place.) The brief initial flexing of the R knee allows the body to pull upward as the knee straightens and the revolution takes place (Ct 5). The lift of the torso, neck, head, and arms, which swing out naturally, should appear breath-filled and suspended like that of a bird in flight. Catching the weight after 1 (or 2) revolutions, step down on the L foot (Ct 6). Now the progression has shifted; by stepping R-L-R, the turn will be executed on the L foot to the left side.

Inside Turns, Suggested Practice

Count and *Tempo:* Same as above.

Stepping forward R-L-R (Cts 1-2-3), transfer the weight from the R foot onto the L leg, bending the L knee and bearing down on the foot briefly (Ct 4), then immediately rising to half-toe for a revolution to the right (Ct 5). R leg is lifted off the floor in a forward direction and held freely in the air for the duration of the turn. The arms swing out naturally as the spin occurs. Step forward on R foot on Ct 6.

Repeat with the L foot initiating the movement phrase, and the turn taking place on the R foot to the left.

Triplets Combined with Turns

To perform the turns which will be used in connection with the Triplets with Turning/Falling Motifs, it is necessary first to practice the sequence with the turns but without the arm coordinations.

Movement Path: Clockwise with turns to the right.

Starting Position: R foot pointed forward, arms at sides. Focus in direction of Movement Path.

Phrases 1-4: Progressing forward 2 triplets, turn on the 3rd triplet to the right, almost in place, making sure that on the 4th triplet, the L foot, in taking the first beat, is stepping backward so that the dancer pivots around to face clockwise again.

Repeat counter-clockwise, making the L turn with reversed foot action.

56. TRIPLETS WITH TURNING/FALLING MOTIFS

Combining the above practice turn with arm movements and the falling pattern described in Exercise 54. The turn is now negotiated with greater ease due to the fact that as the body relaxes into the fall, the impetus for the turn is increased.

Movement Path: Clockwise for R turns and counter-clockwise for L turns.

Starting Position: Upstage left, facing an imaginary circle. R foot pointed forward, arms at sides.

Phrases 1-4: The arms are now used contrapuntally, as in Exercise 54, in the slow 4/4 rhythm against the quick 3/4 rhythm of the feet, with the addition of the turn which is executed on the 3rd and 4th triplet. Progress forward 2 triplets, bringing the arms above the head by the 2nd measure (Ct 2). On Ct 3, start the turn to the right, letting the body and head fall sideways to the left; the arms open sideways in concave curves. As you step back on the L foot (Ct 4), pull the R shoulder to the right in the direction of the turn. In executing this last movement the R arm, as it opens and falls, will drop in front of the body, while the L arm will curve behind the back—the arms behave much as a full skirt might do (wrapping itself around the body) when the wearer spins. At the end of this phrase, you are facing the direction of your advance (clockwise) again and are ready to repeat the entire sequence.

Repeat in a counter-clockwise direction, starting with the L foot and turning left with the combined falling motion of the arms and body sideways-right.

Note: When proficiency (fluency) is gained, the sequence should be danced at a faster tempo.

Variation: For One Arm. Start in the slowest tempo and proceed clockwise. Arms are now lifted above the head and forward of the face in sideways convex curves, palms facing out. Advance 2 triplets without arm change (Cts 1-2). On Ct 3, the L arm *only* falls sideways to the left, dropping the body with it. (The triplets continue with the turning motion on Cts 3-4). On Ct 4, the recovery takes place with the L arm being pulled upward by the body itself; the head recovers last, but the entire movement is completed by the end of the 4th triplet, which brings the body around to advance clockwise again. At the end of the phrase both arms are above the head as at the beginning.

Repeat in a counter-clockwise direction, starting with the L foot and turning left with the body falling sideways-right.

Note: When fluency is gained, the sequence can be danced at a faster tempo.

57. SIDEWAYS LEAPS WITH VARIATIONS

The Humphrey Sideways Leap—used as a lyrical statement in *Passacaglia*—begins with a cross-over step of the foot from which the dancer leaps. In traveling to the right, the L foot crosses over the R foot at a distance of approximately 2" diagonally in advance of the toes of the standing foot (Ct 1). The dancer springs into the air (Ct 2), and lands on the R foot with the knee well-flexed (Ct 3). During the leap, the body remains facing "front," i.e., not twisting toward the right; therefore the leap remains a sideways action. The head, however, is turned in the direction to which the dancer is traveling. Stepping across again with the L foot, a second leap is initiated.

Legs and Feet

The legs and feet are turned out from the hips at a 45-degree angle (a modified First Position) and the standing leg (R) maintains this turn-out as the L foot crosses over. The distance of the cross-over (2") is easily handled with a slight bend in the L knee and a stretch in the R knee (never rigid). The turn-out is maintained on the landing actions as well, the R knee flexing sideways over the R foot, the L knee the same over the L foot.

Arms, Body, and Head

The pelvis and torso maintain correct alignment throughout the action, with a slight, angled lean in the torso in the direction of the leap. When the dancer travels in a circle, the positioning of the body faces "out" on the circle's periphery. When practicing the movement in the other direction, the body changes its frontal position accordingly. The arms are at shoulder height, extended sideways, somewhat forward of the shoulders. The head, turned toward the path of the leap, is neither lifted up nor dropped down. The eyes are focused straight ahead.

Tempo: (3/4 time) Allegro vivace *Music Quality:* Resonant, lyrical, with a fairly strong accent on beat one.

Exercise 57 Sideways Leaps with Variations (Variation I, Count 5): Gail Corbin

Movement Path: For practice, move clockwise in a circle when starting with the L foot, counter-clockwise when starting with the R foot.

Suggested Repetition: Continuous sideways leaps in clockwise direction taking off from the L foot and landing on the R foot. Repeat in counter-clockwise direction, starting with the L foot.

Variation I: Circular Arm Coordination on Every Second Leap. Count in 6s to cover 2 measures (2 leaps). Keeping the arms extended sideways at shoulder height, take the 1st leap from the L foot in a clockwise direction with no change of arm position (Cts 1-3). On the 2nd leap, swing the L arm down to the right across the body on the take-off with the L leg (Ct 4). The arm will reach the zenith of the swing on Ct 5, and be completing the circle as you land on the R foot on Ct 6. Proceed with the same set of movements, coordinating the arm swing on alternate leaps.

Repeat to the left, using the R arm in conjunction with the take-off from the R foot.

Variation II: Three Leaps and a Turn. A phrase of 4 measures divided into 2 sets of 6s, and coming to a climax with a turn. Now combine the 1st leap with the arm swing, taking off from the L foot and swinging the L arm in the circular pattern (Cts 1-3). Do not use the arms on the next leap (Cts 4-6), but hold them out at shoulder height. Leap again, swinging the L arm (Cts 1-3) and upon landing immediately cross the L foot over the R (Ct 4) and make a complete turn to the right on half-toes with a suspension on Ct 5; catch the body's weight by stepping in the direction of the general movement on the R foot (Ct 6) and proceed to repeat the entire phrase.

Repeat in counter-clockwise direction starting with the R foot crossing over the L foot, and the R arm initiating the circular swing on Ct 1.

58. DOUBLE WAVE EXCERPT FROM WATER STUDY

Imagistically conceived, *Water Study*[1] conjures up a variety of sea-moods ranging from calmness to tidal and wind-driven turbulence. Performed in silence, the dance calls for ensemble work of the most subtle and complex order: completely synchronized rhythmic timing between the dancers.

I have chosen the Double Wave Excerpt (the description is mine) from *Water Study* because it combines movements already practiced in Center Work and

Barre Work. Another important reason is that the movement, being performed without music by two groups of dancers at the same time, requires a thorough understanding of rhythm based on the dynamics of the Fall/Recovery principle as applied to successional motion. Four or eight dancers may learn the movement and perform it contrapuntally as it was performed in *Water Study* by two alternating groups.

This excerpt will include six Movement-Phrases executed by two dancers starting from opposite sides of the stage. There are no counts. The dancers' combined movements suggest the confluence of big waves on a stormy sea. They "splash" against each other, break suddenly, and are seemingly sucked downward and backward by an undertow.

Directions will begin with a pulling movement which comes immediately after the two dancers have run from midstage to the far sides of the stage. Facing front and positioning themselves so that a wide swing to the far side will not hit against the stage "wings", they perform the same movements in opposition.

Movement Path: Each group traverses one half of the stage horizontally.

Starting Position: (Directions are for one dancer only; please translate R foot, etc., for L foot, etc., when referring to the movements to be performed by the 2nd dancer.) Dancer on stage left: Legs planted far apart, knees bending in the direction of stage left, torso partially facing front but bending sideways in the direction of stage left, arms at sides rounded to conform with the body's curve. Head turned to stage left and eyes focused on a distant point beyond the "wings."

Movement-Phrase 1: Swing both arms toward stage left with a strong downward emphasis. The movement is like a heavy undertow which sweeps the body sideways and pulls the torso and arms almost in profile. The R leg is stretched from toes to hip; the L knee is well bent with the heel solidly on the floor; the arms are extended toward the "wings."

Movement-Phrase 2: Swing down and back in like manner toward the center of the stage. Both arms are in front of the body and the hips also face stage center. Arms are fully stretched. Immediately following the swing, the legs adjust from their wide spread to the following positions: Upstage (R) foot is in advance of downstage (L) foot and slightly to the side (see Exercise 50: Preparation), the body's weight is on half-toe, and each dancer is facing the other from far across the stage.

Movement-Phrase 3: A circular succession as deep as that practiced at the barre, but with both arms swinging and balancing the body. The dynamics follow the rhythm of a strong backward pull with the body which slows as rising begins to take place and comes to a suspension when the arms reach above the head. This movement is done by the partners in unison and, at the point of suspension, each dancer is looking across the stage sensing the other's readiness to "fall."

Movement-Phrase 4: With a sudden drop over, elbows and hands pulling down close to the body, start running in a crouching position toward your partner (who is running toward you). The run consists of a series of steps starting with the R foot and, depending on the width of the stage, the traveling phrase absorbs approximately 5 running steps (R-L-R-L-R) ending with a jump on both feet (the 6th step), which serves as a preparation for an upward shooting leap into the air opposite your partner. The leap is a take-off from both feet and a landing on one (R). This outflung position in the air brings the partners briefly face to face. (The leap resembles the crest of the wave and the fall, which follows immediately, resembles the wave's sudden "breaking.") From the height of the leap, drop instantly into a side fall to the left by swinging the arms under to catch the body's weight (see Exercise 39).

Movement-Phrase 5: From the prone position of the side fall, pull up sideways by coming to the L hip, which bears the body's weight, crossing the R leg with bent knee over toward stage left, and rising with gathering momentum; the arms are extending sideways now, quite low, and the movement as a whole remains low; the following rush to stage left is in the form of an undertow which, upon the dancer's arrival (the starting point of the Big Wave Excerpt) at the far left, reverses itself acting as a preparation for another swinging motion.

Movement-Phrase 6: A repeat of the 1st Movement-Phrase but slightly faster, due to the fact that the surging movement of the "sea" is gathering more and more momentum.

Note: In *Water Study*, these running-leaping-falling passages are repeated four times (two groups moving in and out twice).

59. 9/8 RHYTHM FROM THE SHAKERS[1]

Whereas *Water Study* deals principally with the smooth articulation of successional flow, the movement vocabulary of *The Shakers* is concerned with sharp, angular, incisive, thrusting motions.

In *The Shakers,* a dance describing the religious practices of an early American sect, the angular, incisive movement takes several forms. First, it is seen as a stiffening of the body when two dancers, a male and a female, rise from kneeling positions to face each other across an imaginary line which divides the stage into equal sides, right and left. Moving upstage along this imaginary line, which serves to segregate the sexes, they begin a jerky sideways step, still looking at each other but not touching. With their hands in front of them at waist height, they commence a flicking, shaking movement, "a shaking away of sin." Fervor increases in intensity as the other dancers cover the stage in symmetrically divided groups. Then all motion is suddenly arrested when The Eldress of the congregation breaks into an ecstatic "speaking of tongues." Dropping on their knees to face her in awe-struck silence, the dancers begin a compulsive ritual of self-purification.

Suddenly, one dancer breaks into a new rhythm. It is a strident half-walk, half-run which seems to dig into the floor. Phrased in a syncopated 9/8 time-pattern, it is picked up by one after another of the dancers until the entire stage seems to be throbbing with the weight-impacted motion of running and falling.

The following directions seek to describe the 9/8 Rhythm as it was performed in the original version of *The Shakers.*

Tempo: Approximately 60   *Suggested Accompaniment:* drum beat.[1]

Movement Path: From stage left (when performed by men dancers) to stage center, and return. From stage right (when performed by women dancers) to stage center and return. Directions given for women.

Starting Position: The dancer, seen in profile from the audience, is facing the center of the stage. Elbows are bent close to the body. Forearms are pulled up tightly in a vertical plane alongside the chest; they are lined up almost parallel to each other with space between. The body is slanting backward from thigh to shoulder, and the position is held firmly, almost stiffly. The head is likewise in a set position at the same angle. Hands loosely fisted.

Spatial Directions, Dynamics, and Footwork

Movement-Phrase: Starting with the L foot, moving forward toward stage center with heavy step and bent knees in a semi-run, step L (Ct 1)-R (Ct "and")-L (Ct 2)-R (Ct "and")-L (Ct 3). On Ct 3-"and", pull the back leg (R) forward close to the L foot and on Ct 4 fall forward on it, bending it sharply and letting the body drop over it. (This movement and Cts 4-"and"-5-"and" are almost identical to Exercise 5, the only difference being in the intensified heaviness of the *Shaker* motion.) On Ct 4-"and", pull up again through a suspension point, bringing the R foot backward in a broader motion, and fall on the R foot on Ct 5, dropping the weight side-back over the leg which is turned out at a 45- to 50-degree angle. Im-

[1]*The Shakers* was scored for Voice, Accordion, and Drum.

mediately rebound, lifting the R leg in a circular pattern high to the right side (Cts [5]-"and"-6). It is a motion which carries the weight-bearing foot to a half-toe position as it pivots the body in a quarter- to half-turn toward the left. As a rebound, the movement has a powerful upward swing which slants the body to the left in off-balance while the R leg scales the air with increasing tension. The path of the movement is now reversed. With the high leg swing and pivot, the dancer is facing stage right toward the rhythm's starting point. On (6)-"and", she catches her weight on the R leg with a falling forward of the body, and, still falling, steps L (Ct 7)-R (Ct "and")-L (Ct 8). There is a rebound on Ct 8, in which the dancer springs into the air (not high), twisting to the right in a half-turn to face stage center again. Land on both feet on Ct 9, ready to repeat the movement-phrase in its entirety.

Upper Torso, Arms, and Head

Movement-Phrase: During the heavy-weighted, 3-Ct, walking-running phrase, in which the torso is firmly slanted backward, the arms are tensely extending from the bent-elbow position into parallel lines stretching forward and diagonally upward, as though in frantic supplication or prayer; by Ct 3-"and", they are in front of the body fully stretched (but not stiff), ready to fall forward and down as the body does so on Ct 4. When this happens, there is a sharp, dramatic overthrow of the body's weight, as if digging into the ground (floor). The rebound on Ct (4)-"and" jerkily straightens the body upward into an arch-shaped suspension, letting the arms hang more or less naturally by the body's sides. This suspension, as we have seen, becomes the crest of another fall, backward. On Ct 5, as the dancer drops side-back, her R shoulder is falling sideways over the turned-out leg, and her R arm is also pulled sideways back. On the rebound from this second fall, the R leg and R arm simultaneously swing upward and outward in a wide circle (Cts 5-6). The leg is at hip height, the arm at shoulder height, but the effect is of a great wheeling motion because the body, by virtue of the counter-clockwise twist of the rebound, swings around, pivoting on the weight-bearing (L) foot, and falling far to the left in an off-balance position. As the leg and arm seem to be shooting out from the hip and shoulder, respectively, the body pulls up sideways on the right, eyes looking up, and the reeling effect (and sensation) is complete. Inevitably, the weight is caught on the R foot on Ct 6-"and", the arm descending as well. Now both arms are hanging, not limply, from the shoulders as the dancer resumes the heavy walking-run on Cts 7-"and"-8 (L-R-L). The arms are tensely held close to the body, alongside the hips. On the concluding jump (Ct 9), both arms spring back into the starting position as though snapped into place along with the slanted body.

Note: Keep the intensity alive in every part of the body, and in the face as well. This is a "rhythmic pattern . . . developed from basic emotional drives,"[1] and the impetus for the action comes from the center of one's being.

60. SIX-COUNT PHRASE FROM PASSACAGLIA

The theme and the structure of Doris Humphrey's monumental work to Johann Sebastian Bach's *Passacaglia and Fugue in C Minor* will be discussed in the final chapter of this book. The movement quality which dominates the work is on a grand scale. The original cast, led by Doris Humphrey and Charles Weidman, numbered twenty-five dancers. Movements sweep across the stage in patterns of great strength and dignity. Yet the overall quality of the choreography is lyrical rather than dramatic.

After the majestic opening statements of the *Passacaglia* themes, fresh rhythms emerge and melodies seem to erupt joyously, one after the other. The following six-count phrases, which have a markedly lyrical feeling, have been selected from this section of *Passacaglia*. For the student who has absorbed the movement quality and the dynamics of the technique, these two phrases, though technically difficult, should present no unsurmountable problems.

First Six-Count Phrase: Leg Work and Directional Motion

Description: A turning and leaping phrase performed in sequences for practice. The steps are on Cts 1, 3, 4, 5, and 6, each phrase starting on the alternate foot.

Movement Path: For purposes of repetition as practice. Travel counter-clockwise with half-turns on the periphery of a large circle, using an arc for each phrase of 6 beats. If the first phrase of 6 beats starts facing the inside of the circle, then the next phrase starts facing out.

Tempo: 112 (Suggested for practice).

Starting Position: (Specific only to the practicing of the movement as an excerpt). Facing the center of the room as though standing on the edge of a circle, weight should be on L foot with R foot poised behind in readiness to step sideways to the right.

Phrase 1: (Counts 1-6.) Stepping on the R foot (Ct 1) and traveling counter-clockwise in the circle, make an inside half-turn toward the left on the R foot, maintaining the turn in a suspension on Ct 2 with the L knee lifted easily in front

---

[1]From descriptive material (excerpt by E.S.) used in the Dance Notation Score of *The Shakers.*

of the body while rotating. The foot should be no higher than the middle of the pivoting thigh. The dancer is now facing out, and continuing to travel counter-clockwise on the periphery of the circle. On Ct 3, step on the L foot to the left, then on the R foot with a cross-over step in front of the L foot (Ct 4), bending the knee and springing into a soft sideways leap with the body still facing out. The R leg extends side-back in the leap, straightening the knee in the process. The leg is turned out, but not up. Turning the L leg out, land on the L foot on Ct 5, then step across with the R foot on Ct 6.

Note: Cts 3-6 are executed on the outer rim of the circle's periphery.

Phrase 2: (Counts 1-6.) Repetition in the same counter-clockwise direction with Cts 3-6 facing the inside of the circle's periphery. Starting with the L foot on Ct 1, make an inside half-turn to the right with a suspension on Ct 2 as the R knee lifts into the air in front of the body while rotating. When the body faces in at the end of the half-turn, step to the right on the R foot on Ct 3, then cross over in front of the R foot with the L foot on Ct 4. Bend the L knee as the leg crosses and spring into the air with a soft sideways leap. Land on the R foot on Ct 5, and cross over the L foot on Ct 6.

First Six-Count Phrase: Arms and Body Motions

Phrase 1: (Counts 1-6.) The arms and body motions change to the opposite side turn, pull sideways-up through the torso to the left, bending the L elbow about ear height. The L hand falls close to the L shoulder. The body bends sharply to the right, the head looking sideways down. The R arm is extended downward on a slant to the right, making a long diagonal line across the body from the L elbow to the R fingers, which may be lightly pressed away from the body. Maintain this position in the turn and do not change the arms throughout the remaining counts on the "cross leap" and land (Cts 3-6).

Phrase 2: (Counts 1-6.) The arms and body motions change to the opposite side on the repeat of the Phrase, stepping on the L foot to turn right, etc. Step on the L foot to execute an inside half-turn to face the inside of the circle. Bend sideways-up on right side of the torso with the arms in the previously described slanting positions (R elbow lifted, at an angle, hand near shoulder, L arm extended downward diagonally). The head, as before, is turned toward the down-slanting arm.

Note: The directions for the body bend emphasize the up-thrust of the torso on the side of the lifted arm rather than the downward pull. This is necessary for

First Six Count Phrase, *Passacaglia* (Count 2): Lane Sayles

smooth execution of the half-turn with its suspension on Ct 2, the lifted action carrying the body around efficiently.

Second Six-Count Phrase

Description: A traveling motion beginning with a sideways succession through the body and arm with a rhythmically corresponding lift of the same leg as the arm, and moving progressively across the room. Facing front, then back, each phrase starts with the alternate foot, stepping on Cts 1, 4, and 6.

Movement Path: Each phrase travels in a straight line across the room from left to right and reverse; the dancer faces front (downstage) with 1st set of 6 beats, then faces back (upstage) with the 2nd set of 6 beats. (For additional range within a given space, work the movement diagonally through the studio.)

Tempo: 112 (Suggested for practice).

Starting Position: (Specific only to practicing the movement as an excerpt). Facing front, far left side of room, weight on R foot, L foot turned out, crossed in front of R to step on Ct 1; arms dropped easily at the sides, body held without stiffness, focus forward.

Phrase 1: (Counts 1-3.) Step across onto L foot, bend the L knee and begin a rippling sideways succession (see Exercise 2) upward through the R arm and torso tilting the body far over to the left in a falling motion (Cts 1-3). *Do not hold back on the sideways falling; it should be tilted radically to the side with a sense of abandon.* During these counts, the R leg follows the successional pattern by lifting the knee sideways up, then the foreleg and foot until the angle of the R leg parallels that of the R arm. By Ct 3 the body is falling sideways to the left on an acute angle, with the head turned sideways-up, the eyes looking past the R hand, and the L foot on half-toe.

   (Counts 4-6.) An emphatic change takes place on Ct 4: A quick recovery from the sideways falling motion brings the body up through center, then over to the right with a sharp waist bend as weight is shifted to the R foot (on half-toe), and the R hand, turned sideways, presses inward parallel to legs and thighs with the palm leading. The torso is lifted upward as the body bends right, R shoulder tilted downward on its own side. The L arm stays close to the left side of the body in a natural curve paralleling the torso pull. The face is turned sideways to look forward past the R shoulder and the L leg is swung across the R leg with a slight lift (bend) in the L knee. All this occurs on Ct 4, with a breath-filled suspension of the same movement taking place on Ct 5. Step across on the L foot (half-toe) on Ct 6, letting the body continue to fall right through the R shoulder and waist, during which motion the R hand begins to relax as does the body in preparation for a repeat of the phrase to the left side.

Repeat, taking a half-turn on the R foot as the succession through the left side of the body begins, the fall occurring to the right. Proceed with the above directions reversed.

Note: The phrase should be repeated until a freedom is established and the falling motif becomes clearer and more daring with practice. The body's support on the standing leg, which is always in flux, is secured through the "wholeness" of the movement, with its energy flow reaching a climax by Ct 3 of the initial succession.

Second Six-Count Phrase, *Passacaglia* (Count 3): Carla Maxwell

Second Six-Count Phrase, *Passacaglia* (Count 4): Carla Maxwell

PART THREE

THE CREATIVE POTENTIAL OF THE TECHNIQUE

The technique evolved out of this theory
is amazingly rich in possibilities.
   Doris Humphrey

Chapter 7
CLASSROOM RESOURCES

INTRODUCTION

From the beginning of a lesson until its conclusion, mind and body are at work in the pursuit of an esthetic ideal. It will be a hard-won ideal, achieved only through persistent mental and physical effort, otherwise known as discipline. To quote Nietzsche: "It is no small advantage to have a hundred Damoclean swords suspended above one's head; that is how one learns to dance, that is how one attains 'freedom of movement.' "[1]

The end product of such discipline, after a substantial amount of time, should be fluency of motion, faultless rhythmic coordination, and superb muscular control. Quite a roster of accomplishments! Add to these, a well-developed sensitivity to music and a temperament that delights in visceral experience, and our well-trained terpsichorean comes close to perfection. Yet, for the dedicated dancer, the most gratifying experience lies ahead: the creative use of the technique.

In her credo, quoted in part at the end of Chapter 2, Doris Humphrey describes her vision of the dance as based on "reality illumined by imagination." If we consider reality to be the evidence of what we see, hear, feel, touch, and smell in the everyday world, then natural movement as we experience and observe it is

---

[1] Nietzsche, *Der Wille zur Macht* (IN: Havelock Ellis, *The Dance of Life.* New York: The Modern Library, 1929), p. 265.

assuredly empirical proof of reality. Consequently, the theories derived from natural movement, upon which the Humphrey Technique is based, have the power to serve as fecund sources of inspiration for the future dancer/choreographer.

In presenting the movement vocabulary of the Humphrey Technique, we have already taken the initial step in exploring the technique's rich potential by enlarging the scope of many exercises through "variations" and the introduction of new choreographic forms. An example of the latter is the Figure Eight series (Exercises 20-21). In essence, the Figure Eight sequences are transformations of the preceding Swing series (Exercises 14-19), through intensification of the dynamic action inherent in the Swing, varying the rhythmic pulse, and changing the overall design. Note that the principles of Fall and Recovery still operate as the chief ingredients in the new structure; in fact, they are even more clearly seen in the Figure Eights because the image has doubled.

When used imaginatively, Rhythm, Dynamics, and Design—classified by Doris Humphrey as the three basic ingredients of dance movement—have the power to create patterns of infinitely varied textures. Let us examine them separately in relation to a specific Humphrey principle: Change of Weight.

VARIATION IN RHYTHM

Taking the Walking Version of Change of Weight (Exercise 4), alter the 4/4 rhythm to a 9/8 rhythm in the following manner:

Rhythmic Count: In 9s, with a suspension on Ct 3. Retain the forward and backward falling motif, but combine them now into one phrase.

Movement Path: A diagonal traversing of the dance area.

Tempo: Approximately 88.

Starting Position: Facing downstage-right corner. Weight on L foot, R foot pointed forward in readiness for a step on Ct 1. L arm lifted forward in opposition; R arm slightly to the rear (also in opposition).

Phrase: Step forward on R foot (Ct 1), swing L leg gently forward with oppositional swing of R arm (Ct 2). Arms are about waist height and the knee of the lifted leg is bent slightly at hip height with foreleg and foot pointed slantingly downward. A suspension hold on Ct 3 which pulls the body forward causing the heel of the R foot to rise from the floor as the weight travels through the body.

Fall forward 3 steps catching your weight on the L foot on Ct 4, then again on the R foot on Ct 5, and on the L again on Ct 6. (The movement is the same as Exercise 4 on Cts 3-"and"-4). Regaining balance, pull up and back by stepping backward onto the R leg on Ct 7. The body is now almost upright, but the backward pull is still taking effect and the next movement is another drop backward on the L leg (which is well turned out for proper support) to catch the weight on Ct 8. Rebound onto the R foot with a strong recovery which brings you upward through the arc of the movement on Ct 9. You are now ready to repeat the rhythm, starting with the L leg.

Note: Arms. Throughout the above sequence, the arms fall naturally with the body as it moves, once the oppositional swing has taken place, arms remain relaxed alongside the body very much as in the original Change of Weight: Walking Version.

VARIATION IN DYNAMICS

Using the same Walking Version of Change of Weight, alter the dynamics drastically by shifting the direction from forward-back to sideways. The sequence will now involve an extreme off-balance pull in which each leg is extended by turns to its own side high in the air while the body, outflung in the opposite direction, tries to maintain equilibrium at an oblique angle.

Rhythmic Count: In 8s, with holds on Cts 2 and 6.

Movement Path: A straight line from stage left to stage right, traversing space horizontally.

Tempo: Same as above.

Starting Position: Facing front, weight on L leg, arms at sides, R leg crossed behind L in readiness to step sideways to the right.

Phrase: With impulse on "and", cross the arms in front of the body and step to the right on R foot with bent knee, sending the L leg high into the air in a sideways extension, and tilting the body sideways to the far right; simultaneously swing the arms to a wide open position at shoulder height. The body is now slanting radically in a completely extended position which is angled sharply as though it is falling. The spine remains straight but the head is turned toward the left, looking upward in the direction of the L hand. All this occurs on Ct 1. Maintain the tilted suspension-extension with, if possible, a sense of further falling to the right (Ct 2). Now step across the R foot with the L foot (Ct 3) bending the L knee and still slanting the body to the far right as though still falling. In the same

tilted position, step to the right again on Ct 4. With a radical shift in body position, cross the L foot *in back* of the R on Ct 5 and tilt the entire body to the left
with a leg thrust similar to that of Ct 1. In the act of changing weight on Cts 3-4,
the arms drop naturally with the body into a crossed position in front of the torso with the back slightly rounded; on Ct 5, they swing out again to coordinate
with and maintain the high suspension-extension of the R leg on Ct 6 while the
body slants radically to the left. They are, as in Cts 1-2, extended at shoulder
height, and the head is now turned toward the right, looking upward in the direction of the R hand. On Ct 7, step sideways to the right on the R foot, pulling upward with the body and gradually regaining balance. Arms remain in sideways
position, but react with the body to the gravitational pull. With another sideways
step on Ct 8—crossing the L foot in front of the R foot—balance restored, arms
are dropping into the crossed position, and you are now ready to repeat the movement. In reversing directions, start on the L foot to the left and bend left, etc.

Note: On both sideways extensions (Cts 2 and 6), the positioning of shoulders,
hips, and extended leg is maintained in one plane. Avoid hips buckling.

VARIATION IN DESIGN

Combining the above Rhythmic and Dynamic Variations in sequences of three
phrases for the first and two phrases for the second, a new format may be introduced to change the movement pattern directionally. It is understood, of course,
that bodily design changes occur spontaneously, as do dynamic variations, as soon
as rhythmic changes are incorporated into a movement. However, we are consider-
ing here spatial design mainly in terms of a floor plan.

 Starting from upstage left on the L foot, perform three phrases of the Rhythmic Variation in 9/8 time on a diagonal line crossing stage center. Changing to
the Dynamic Variation with the Sideways pattern, move upstage right starting
with the R foot in the 8-Ct phrase, which is danced twice. At the end of 2nd
phrase, when stepping across on the L foot on Ct 8, pivot to the right on the L
foot to face the downstage-left corner to start the repeat of the 1st sequence of
9 Counts on the R foot. Proceed in a diagonal line for 3 phrases of 9s, at the end
of which the weight is on the R foot. Shifting again to the Dynamic Variation
with the Sideways pattern, move upstage left starting on the L foot in the 8-Ct
phrase. At the end of the 2nd phrase, when stepping across on the R foot on Ct
8, pivot to the left on the R foot to face the downstage-right corner. You are
now in a position to repeat the entire sequence.

Note: Arm movements on the pivots will naturally swing with the body as it ro-
tates to face the opposite corner.

VARIATIONS IN THE FORM OF A STUDY

Selecting Figure Eights: Alternate Sides (Exercise 20), let us see how a fairly simple exercise can be extended into an increasingly complex series of movement which could develop into a Study— a Study being a miniature dance composition. By expanding the movement of the Sideways Figure Eight spatially and dynamically through a rephrasing of the movement into a horizontal traveling pattern, the dancer weaves across the studio from one end to the other. The introduction of a syncopated rhythm, of one turn or more at a given point, and an increase in tempo and intensity would suggest an elaboration of the original Figure Eight pattern. This secondary theme could be intercepted at a given point by movements of contrasting design and dynamics, which would alter the spatial directions. Then, with a resumption of the Figure Eight pattern on a smaller scale, more concentrated, tighter forms could "erupt" at a greater speed, the whole building to a climax in which a jump or a fall (or both) would bring the sequence to a conclusion. No formula, of course, is intended in this brief sugges-

Circular Arms: Penelope Hill

tion; only an offering of a hypothetical example of imaginative play on pure movement themes. In similar manner, Successions, Swings, Falls, Running, Leaping, etc., provide inspirational starting points for endless choreographic innovations along individual creative paths.

That such paths undoubtedly lead to new insights, new material, and new dance forms was already anticipated with typical open-mindedness by Doris Humphrey when she visualized ever-changing dance forms in an ever-changing world and jotted down these notes, which, in excerpt form, read like a prophecy in free verse:[1]

> As one critic has stated
> Every reason to believe
> There will always be an indigenous American Dance
> Known to the period as modern
> It does not matter if there is no one system which endures
> Indeed this is advantage
> For without crystallization there is chance for growth . . .
> I believe . . . that America is overflowing with themes and creative talent
> That there will be and should be dancers
> In the American style from the plains
> From the cities—mountains
> South north east west
> Each with a vital contribution
> Made in America. . . .

[1] Doris Humphrey Collection. Folder M-58.

Humphrey Dynamics, Extension-Suspension: Penelope Hill

Movement from *A Choreographic Offering* (José Limón) inspired by and based on dances of Doris Humphrey: Lane Sayles

Movement from *A Choreographic Offering* (José Limón) inspired by and based on dances of Doris Humphrey : Lane Sayles

Epilogue
CHOREOGRAPHIC CONCEPTS

Air for the G String was the opening dance on the historic occasion of the first independent appearance of Doris Humphrey, Charles Weidman, and the Concert Group as a performing unit. The date was October 28, 1928; the locale, the Civic Repertory Theatre on West 14th Street, New York City.

Studied retrospectively, *Air for the G String,* set to Johann Sebastian Bach's serenely soaring "Air on the G String" from his *Orchestral Suite No. 3 in D Minor,* can be viewed as early evidence of Doris Humphrey's innate belief in "the nobility that the human spirit is capable of. . . ." One might even say that the choreographic concept behind this smoothly flowing quintet anticipated the artist's later identification with the Nietzschean vision of the Apollonian-Dionysian elements in man. In *Air for the G String,* there is not one broken, erratic gesture. The entire dance expresses an Apollonian dream image in which a "philosophical calmness" moves the mind. The quiet legato movements of the five dancers ascend and descend in rhythmic accord with the long sustained phrases of the music; and the gentle intertwining of the central figure with the four novitiates of this seemingly perfect world suggests her role as spiritual leader. The costumes, with their voluminous gold scarves trailing behind the dancers occasionally revealing the magenta-pink and celestial blue of the sheath-like dresses beneath, remind one of the colors and forms of angelic representations in the religious paintings of the fifteenth-century Florentine master, Fra Angelico.

Doris Humphrey's choice of Bach's music as the symbolic voice of such idealistic visions had its roots, we are told by the choreographer herself, in her first hearing of the "Air on the G String" as a child: she was "struck . . . to the heart."[1] Into this short dance, with its stately processions and symmetrical groupings, the choreographer poured all the lyricism of a nature which could "conceive in passion and execute in reason."[2] Hers, indeed, was the "pure, undimmed eye" which could visualize, according to Nietzsche, "Apollonian perfection." The real wonder lies in the fact that *Air for the G String* was the forerunner by three years of the choreographer's discovery of the German philosopher's theory of mankind's intermingling impulses.[3]

To the average theatergoer in 1930, Doris Humphrey's *Choreographic Valse,* the short-lived title for the ballet later known as *La Valse,* may well have seemed to be a straight reenactment of a mid-nineteenth century European ballroom scene. Costumed in formal evening attire, the eighteen dancers, including Doris Humphrey and Charles Weidman, performed vigorous German ländlers (a precursor of the waltz) and swirling Viennese waltzes to Maurice Ravel's symphonic poem, "La Valse."

Yet, there was something curiously disturbing in the way the ballet ended. As if the imaginary ballroom's crystal chandeliers were suddenly shattered and the debris lay everywhere, a wild licentiousness took place when all the dancers, save the leading pair, threw themselves madly across the stage, plunging into falls as the music came to a final, screeching halt. Transfixed, stage center, the remaining couple looked about them in shocked disdain at their companions' reckless behavior.

Another eerie touch was provided in the ballet's quasi-savage opening, which conveyed the same ominous atmosphere as that

[1] Humphrey, *The Art of Making Dances.* p. 19.
[2] Leonardo da Vinci, often quoted by D.H.
[3] Fortunately, there is an unusually sensitive film of *Air for the G String* (Westinghouse, 1934) which conveys the Apollonian atmosphere of the dance as performed against a background representing the multi-columned arches of a medieval cathedral. The key, however, to the composition's lyricism is to be found in Doris Humphrey's luminous performance in the leading role.

suggested in the first witches scene in *Macbeth*. Massed together on the floor in semi-darkness, indistinguishable forms rose and fell intermittently like sporadic flames from a smoldering fire. Sinister implications these; possibly too elusive for audiences unaccustomed to view the dance as something more profound than mere "entertainment."

One spectator who did perceive the underlying choreographic intention of *La Valse* was John Martin, at that time the little-known dance critic for the *New York Times*. In his review the following day (January 7, 1930), Martin spoke of Doris Humphrey's *Choreographic Waltz* as a composition in which ". . . she and Mr. Weidman and the ensemble gave an extremely decadent picture of a pseudo-Empire bacchanale." With typical acuity, the critic recognized the choreographer's attempt to depict a society in the last throes of moral disintegration.

Was *La Valse* another instance of Doris Humphrey's unconscious divination of the fundamental truth of man's duality as described in Nietzsche's *The Birth of Tragedy?* Seen from this vantage point, the "bacchanale" implicit in the finale of *La Valse* could conceivably be interpreted as a nineteenth century Dionysian escape into the revelry of the dance. Certainly, Ravel's music was an expression of man's "unquenchable desire for excitement," the phrase used by Doris Humphrey to describe the Dionysian element in human nature.[1] The story goes that Ravel himself became intoxicated with the rhythms of the Viennese waltz, and that once commited to the writing of "La Valse," "he lived in a fever of excitement."[2]

Both the choreographic and musical "scenarios" would indicate that the primitive beginning of *La Valse* contained the seeds of its fatalistic ending. Only the center section of this twelve-minute work sought to convey the conventional delights of dancing the waltz, and even in these passages there is a macabre gaiety that possesses the music and the dancers. Like the weird mutterings of the witches in *Macbeth*, the images of the amorphous forms return to plague us.

In the mysterious, murky opening scene, men and women seem to be inextricably woven together. Scraps of rhythm issue from the depths of a pianissimo introduction as human forms emerge momentarily and then are pulled back into the matted center.

[1] Humphrey, *The Art of Making Dances.* p. 56.
[2] Victor I. Seroff, *Maurice Ravel* (New York: Holt, 1953), p. 210.

Gradually, as if materializing out of the shadows, individuals appear. They begin to dance with peasant-like gusto. Then the men bow courteously to the women, who seem to have suddenly become paragons of virtue and elegance. An exquisitely dressed couple present themselves. She wears an Empire gown of glistening pink silk; he, a frilly white cravat and a black velvet jacket with a high-standing collar.

The waltz begins. Now the dancers assume the proper stance: each man holding his partner's waist at the small of the back with the right hand while extending his left arm far to the side to clasp the lady's outstretched fingers. Movements become more sensual as the couples weave among themselves, encircling the stage. Bending from the waist, the women drop backward as the men swing around them; then they, in turn, swing around the men. The pace quickens. A powerful centrifugal force seems to be taking effect; in a few minutes the entire scene is shimmering with twirling, bobbing revellers who are intoxicated with the rhythm of the waltz. Madness possesses them, and all conventions disappear. Exhilaration has changed to exuberance, exuberance to compulsive excitement; mounting to a climax, the music and the dance end in dissonance and dissolution. Dionysus has triumphed.

Doris Humphrey's solo suite entitled *Two Ecstatic Themes* was the immediate creative result of her 1931 trip to the West Indies. The solos were, as we now know, the most personal lyrical statements of her career. They reflected the stimulation she had found in her Caribbean experience, not only through reading Friedrich Nietzsche's *The Birth of Tragedy* and Havelock Ellis's *The Dance of Life,* but in meeting the man with whom she would eventually share her life. Like love sonnets, they conveyed deep feeling.

Two Ecstatic Themes was premiered at the Washington Irving High School on East 16th Street, Manhattan, on October 31, 1931, in a program that was part of an annual series offering modern dance companies the opportunity to perform their latest works prior to the all-important uptown concerts. The public at these series was wonderfully receptive. I remember the auditorium as being immense, the stage exceedingly wide. Doris's slender figure alone in the center of such enormous space was an impressive sight as the stage lights came up. Clad in a long, white dress, she stood upright facing the audience, her arms outstretched at shoulder height, her legs firmly planted apart. With that steely strength of hers, she seemed invincible—and she was, until the first chords of Nicholas Medtner's romantic *Tragedie-Fragment in A Minor* reverberated through the expectant silence, and the straight lines of her fragile-looking form began to curve languorously into the spiraling designs of *Circular Descent.*

Exquisitely crafted, *Circular Descent* and *Pointed Ascent* (the latter set to the more modern music of the contemporary Italian composer, Gian Francesco Malipiero) were, in comparison with the large-scale *Dionysiaques,* solo declarations of Doris's newly emerging theory of Fall and Recovery. Each dance acted as a metaphor in itself: the curving, falling forms of the first suggested the intoxicating experience of Dionysian release; the aggresive thrust of the second suggested a frantic attempt to regain the security of Apollonian stability. *Two Ecstatic Themes* made a concise, eloquent avowal of the dual philosophical theme that Doris had converted into a movement language of her own. The title, too, had roots in the Nietzschean concept—"ecstatic" obviously referred to that rhapsodic condition of Dionysian off-balance, when "gestures bespeak enchantment."[1]

A further clue is provided in Doris Humphrey's own evaluation of her solos, printed in a program note:

> *Two Ecstatic Themes* is the keynote to Miss Humphrey's mature work. The first part is in circular and spiral movements, soft and sinking, to convey an emotional feeling of acquiescence. The second part, in contrast to the first, moves in pointed design to a strident climax suggestive of aggressive achievement. The whole is a counterpoint of circular and angular movement, representing the two inseparable elements of life as well as of design.[2]

With its multiple rhythms and sweeping designs, the structure of Doris Humphrey's *Passacaglia* resembles the architecture of a resplendent cathedral. Choreographically, its concept of a man-made utopia matches the grandeur of Bach's glorious music, described by Leopold Stokowski as "one of the most divinely inspired contrapuntal works ever conceived." A vision of an ideal

[1] F. Nietzsche, *The Birth of Tragedy,* p. 25.
[2] Program, Repertory Theatre, Boston, Mass., March 14, 15, 1935.

world where the inhabitants live in peaceful accord with one another, *Passacaglia* expresses the choreographer's conviction that man is potentially capable of creating such a utopia. Three years before, Doris Humphrey had composed *New Dance,* which sought to represent "the world as it should be, where each person has a clear and harmonious relationship to his fellow beings."[1]   Now her vision took the form of a magnificent procession (the Passacaglia) followed by an energetic dance (the Fugue) affirming man's ultimate nobility of spirit.

Passacaglia created a mood of serenity coupled with great strength of purpose. It often succeeded in lifting audiences to its visionary heights; but just as often the significance of its abstract symbolism soared above those spectators who either felt that the music overpowered the dance or who failed to relate to such lofty philosophical concepts. The choreographer was well aware of this occasional lack of rapport between her composition and the audience, and mentioned it in a letter describing the experience of performing *Passacaglia* on a 1939 country-wide tour she made with the Humphrey-Weidman Company:

> It was daring to take the *Passacaglia* out with us, playing it impartially to Oklahoma and Boston and the rest. This dance bore the serious message of the program, with Bach, of all things as its purveyor. To the layman Bach is dull; to the sophisticated dancer—dated; to the educated musician—sacrosanct. To whom could we play then, in a dance to Bach, laden with a philosophical meaning? Yet we did win a great many who perhaps did not understand it, who could not possibly have followed the intricacies of the Fugue at first seeing, but who caught something of the nobility and despairing courage of the mood. In the early part of the tour I tried to explain what this dance is about in program notes—"man's reiteration of faith stated in the entries of the Fugue," "his belief in living despite an imperfect world." . . .The dance never failed to lift me up, from fatigue or depression or petty distractions, and also terrified me, as my part called particularly for calm and poise perched high on a box or within inches of the footlights. The choreographer made it hard for herself! How much better to have brought *With My Red Fires,* obvious and crude in comparison, but easy to understand —dramatic, with a plot and characters—much more what people

[1] Doris Humphrey Collection. Folder M-25.

have learned to expect from the dance. . . .Nevertheless, I think *Passacaglia* my most mature dance, with the finest choreography so far.[1]

To perform Doris Humphrey's *Passacaglia* "requires skill, poetry, and nobility,"[2] the attributes of the choreographer, whose imagination and philosophical insights matched her creative gifts.

After *Passacaglia* (1938), no less than twenty-nine dances would be choreographed by Doris Humphrey before her death in 1958. Of these, twelve would be created for the Humphrey-Weidman Company, thirteen for the José Limón Dance Company, and four for the Juilliard Dance Theatre, an ensemble she founded as a member of the faculty of The Juilliard School. Her search for new forms to express ever-surging ideas never abated.

While the compositions set on the Humphrey-Weidman Company included such fine works as *Song of the West* and the gripping *Inquest* (in which Doris danced for the last time), the most innovative choreography of these later years was created for the José Limón dancers, for whom Doris served as Artistic Director from 1946-1958. Inspired by working with a small ensemble of exceptional performers—José, Letitia Ide, Pauline Koner, Betty Jones, Ruth Currier, Lavina Nielson, Lucas Hoving— she let her imagination range over a wide variety of subjects. Foremost among these cameo-like compositions was *Lament for Ignacio Sanchez Mejias,* a subtle blend of recited poetry, music, and movement. Cast for two dancers and an actress, the composition transformed Federico García Lorca's elegiac poem into a dramatic theater piece set against a darkly evocative musical background by Norman Lloyd. On the hard edge of cynicism, *Ruins and Visions* still clung to a typical Humphrey conclusion: humanistic affirmation. The lusty, sophisticated *Ritmo Jondo* used a Spanish setting for its playful juxtaposition of male and female attitudes towards sex and love. Perhaps the most deeply human statement was made in *Day on Earth* with its abiding sense of man's dependence on work, love, and family; while the most ethereal mood was con-

---

[1] Letter from Doris Humphrey, "Thoughts at the Finish of the Tour," written to members of the Humphrey-Weidman Company and other dance associates. Courtesy of Anne MacNaughton.

[2] José Limón, quoted in Labanotation score of *Passacaglia.* (New York: The Dance Notation Bureau).

veyed in *Night Spell* with its haunting images conjuring up a dreamer's world of terror and desire.

Did Doris Humphrey ever feel a lack of ideas, or a sudden scarcity of movement materials? I doubt it. I remember one conversation in the 1950s in which she spoke as enthusiastically as ever of the "endless possibilities" of human movement. Natural movement would again serve her as it had been serving her for nearly thirty years . . . and as it still does for dancers and choreographers who have been inspired by the philosophy and style she established through her technique.

Primary among those who felt indebted to Doris Humphrey was José Limón. Openly grateful, he created *A Choreographic Offering* in which he ingeniously threaded together themes of Doris's dances of earlier years: *Dionysiaques, The Pleasures of Counterpoint, Air on a Ground Bass, Two Ecstatic Themes* and *Passacaglia,* to mention a few. Other disciples still making contributions in one form or another to the dance are Eleanor King, Sybil Shearer, Katherine Litz, Harriet Ann Gray, Nona Schurman, and Beatrice Seckler.

And there are younger artists whose creative efforts speak clearly of a direct line of descent: Carla Maxwell, principal dancer with the José Limón Dance Company; Daniel Lewis, former assistant to José and now director of the Contemporary Dance System; Jennifer Muller, and Louis Falco. The last two still draw upon their extensive training in the Humphrey-Limón tradition. Muller is a superior craftsman when it comes to enlarging the dynamic range of the style. Her intricate patterns are charged with an abandon that is typically Dionysian. Falco, also, has taken the technique to exciting extremes in his own way.

The young are the carriers. To them, Doris Humphrey willingly and freely gave of the fruits of her mind, believing that creativity, when disciplined, is man's most magnificent gesture.

Doris Humphrey in Square Dance (Waltz)